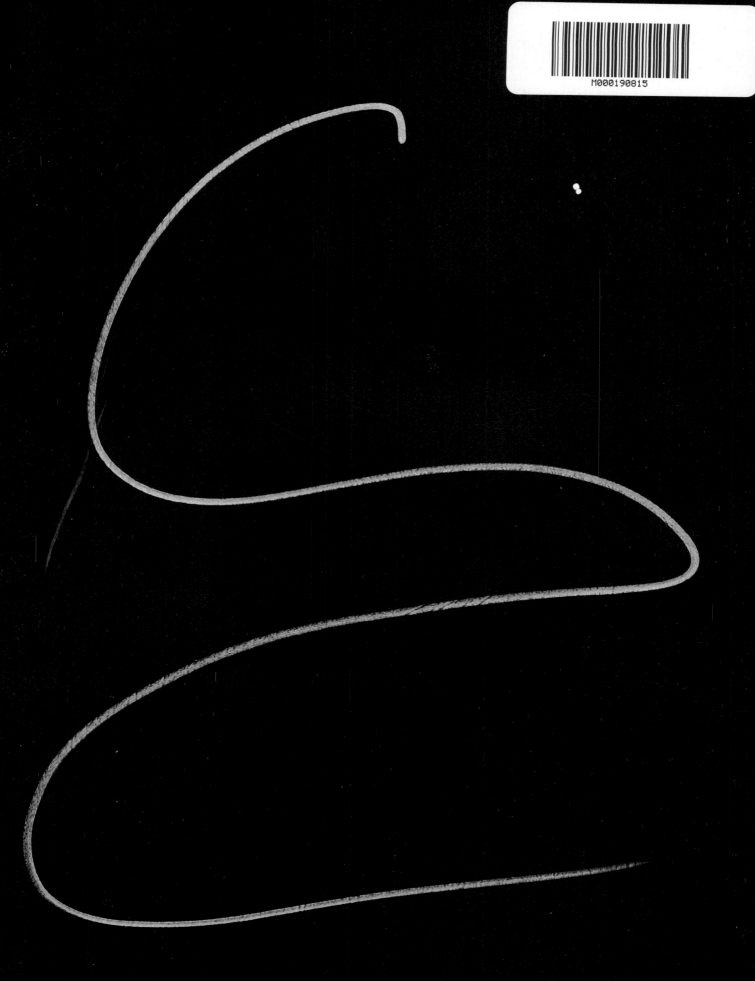

# THE AZUSA STREET

# REVIVAL

## THE HOLY SPIRIT IN AMERICA 100 YEARS

## SPECIAL CENTENNIAL EDITION

**Charisma HOUSE**

A STRANG COMPANY

Most STRANG COMMUNICATIONS/CHARISMA HOUSE/SILOAM/REALMS/
FRONTLINE products are available at special quantity discounts for bulk
purchase for sales promotions, premiums, fund-raising, and educational
needs. For details, write Strang Communications/Charisma House/Siloam/
Realms/FrontLine, 600 Rinehart Road, Lake Mary, Florida 32746,
or telephone (407) 333-0600.

THE AZUSA STREET REVIVAL—SPECIAL CENTENNIAL EDITION
Eddie Hyatt, Author
Joel Kilpatrick, General Editor
Terry Clifton, Designer

Published by Charisma House
A Strang Company
600 Rinehart Road
Lake Mary, Florida 32746
www.charismahouse.com

Library of Congress  Cataloging-in-Publication Data:
Hyatt, Eddie L.
   The Azusa Street revival : the Holy Spirit in America : 100 years
/ Eddie Hyatt. -- Special centennial ed.
      p. cm.
   ISBN 1-59185-790-2 (hardback)
   1. Pentecostalism--United States--History.    I. Title.
BR1644.5.U6H93 2006
277.3'082--dc22
2006001819

First Edition

06 07 08 09 10 — 987654321
Printed in the United States of America

# CONTENTS

# INTRODUCTION

**NEW FAITH**
*A water baptism at Newton Lake in Pennsylvania in the 1920s. On the right, wearing a suit, is J.R. Flower, a longtime leader in the Assemblies of God.*

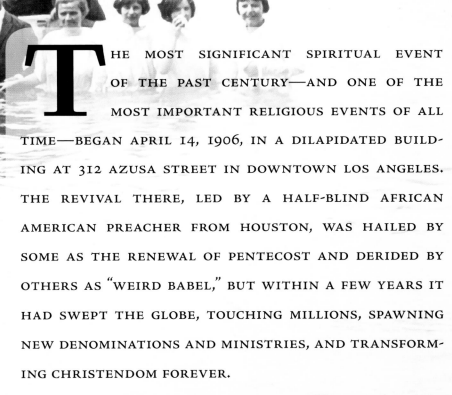

THE MOST SIGNIFICANT SPIRITUAL EVENT OF THE PAST CENTURY—AND ONE OF THE MOST IMPORTANT RELIGIOUS EVENTS OF ALL TIME—BEGAN APRIL 14, 1906, IN A DILAPIDATED BUILDING AT 312 AZUSA STREET IN DOWNTOWN LOS ANGELES. THE REVIVAL THERE, LED BY A HALF-BLIND AFRICAN AMERICAN PREACHER FROM HOUSTON, WAS HAILED BY SOME AS THE RENEWAL OF PENTECOST AND DERIDED BY OTHERS AS "WEIRD BABEL," BUT WITHIN A FEW YEARS IT HAD SWEPT THE GLOBE, TOUCHING MILLIONS, SPAWNING NEW DENOMINATIONS AND MINISTRIES, AND TRANSFORMING CHRISTENDOM FOREVER.

Today, the Pentecostal-Charismatic movement that sprang from the unlikely prayer meeting at Azusa Street counts 600 million followers worldwide and growing. It is "Christianity's fastest growing branch" and continues to shape the church at large. According to a 1998 *Newsweek* poll, nearly half of all Christians in the United States say they have "personally experienced the Holy Spirit," and three-quarters of all evangelical Protestants make the same claim.[1] These pages tell the story of the revival that began at Azusa Street and how in a single century this spiritual brushfire has revolutionized the Christian experience.

# William Seymour and the Azusa Street Revival

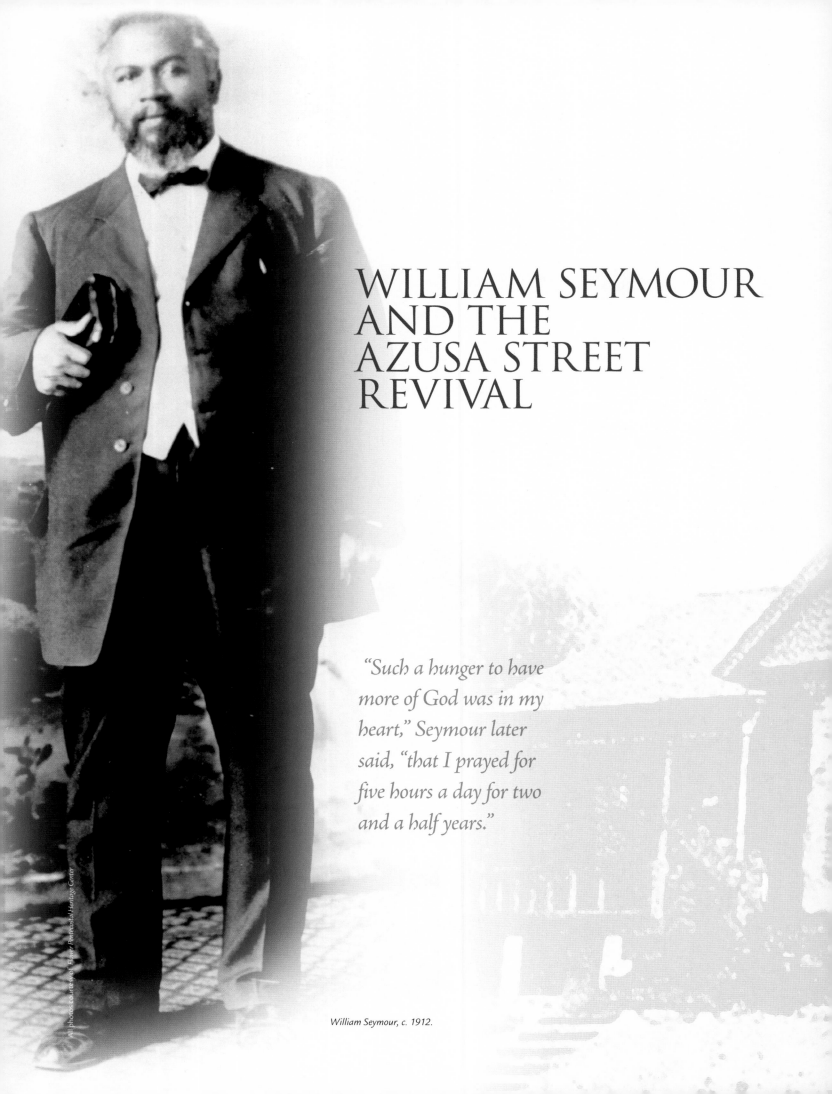

# WILLIAM SEYMOUR AND THE AZUSA STREET REVIVAL

*"Such a hunger to have more of God was in my heart," Seymour later said, "that I prayed for five hours a day for two and a half years."*

William Seymour, c. 1912.

**M**ANY LEADERS EMERGED FROM THE AZUSA STREET REVIVAL, BUT THE MOST SIGNIFICANT PERSON ASSOCIATED WITH THE REVIVAL ITSELF WAS THE SON OF FORMER SLAVES, WILLIAM JOSEPH SEYMOUR. SEYMOUR WAS BORN IN 1870 IN CENTERVILLE, LOUISIANA, AND WAS RAISED IN THE LOCAL BAPTIST CHURCH. AS A BOY HE WAS SPIRITUALLY INCLINED AND HAD MYSTICAL EXPERIENCES, DREAMS AND VISIONS. AS AN ADULT, SMALLPOX LEFT HIM BLIND IN HIS LEFT EYE. TO THOSE WHO KNEW HIM, SEYMOUR WAS A MAN OF UNCOMMON SPIRITUAL HUNGER.

In 1895, when he was twenty-five, Seymour moved to Indianapolis and worked as a waiter in a fashionable restaurant, but in 1900 he moved to Cincinnati and discovered holiness teachings through the Church of God (Anderson, Indiana), known then as the "Evening Light Saints." They taught that a second work of grace called *sanctification* would eradicate the power of "inbred sin" in a believer's life, a doctrine preached by John Wesley in the eighteenth century. Seymour embraced this teaching and moved to Houston in 1903. There he began attending a black Holiness church pastored by Lucy Farrow, the niece of the famous abolitionist Frederick Douglass. "Such a hunger to have more of God was in my heart," Seymour later said, "that I prayed for five hours a day for two and a half years."

Those prayers would soon show great effect.

## LUCY FARROW

Lucy Farrow was born in slavery in Norfolk, Virginia, and distinguished herself as a teacher, preacher, and missionary in early Pentecostalism. Many received the baptism in the Holy Spirit through the laying on of her hands. She departed Los Angeles in August 1906 on her way to Liberia, West Africa, from which her ancestors had been brought to America. Stopping in Houston, she was invited by Charles Parham to preach at his camp meeting in progress. As she preached and shared about the revival in Los Angeles, the power of God fell, and many were baptized in the Holy Spirit. One of the participants, Howard Goss, who became a prominent leader in the movement, said she demonstrated "an unusual power to lay hands on people for the reception of the Holy Spirit."

That a black woman preached to a white audience in the segregated South in 1906 demonstrates the power of the Azusa Street revival to break color barriers, although at times temporarily. After returning to Los Angeles from Liberia, West Africa, in fall 1907, Farrow spent the remainder of her life in a small "faith cottage" behind the Azusa Street Mission where she ministered to many who sought her prayers.

**MAN WITH A MESSAGE**
*A revival poster (left) announced Parham's special meetings in Kansas and Missouri. Parham had "just returned from several month's [sic] research work all over the Holy Land," the poster says. "Mr. Parham is a rare student of prophecy."*

**SPREADING THE WORD**
*Charles Parham (right) with song leader Fred Campbell at Perryton, Texas, in the 1920s.*

**STONE'S FOLLY**
*Site of Charles Parham's Bethel Bible College in Topeka, Kansas (c. 1901). There, Parham and the students experienced a dramatic outpouring of the Holy Spirit during which virtually everyone present spoke in tongues.*

# SEYMOUR MEETS CHARLES PARHAM

In summer 1905, Charles F. Parham, a white Holiness preacher, came to Houston and conducted a citywide crusade in Bryan Hall. Parham had begun preaching a controversial third blessing after sanctification, which he called *the baptism in the Holy Spirit*. He and the students at his Bethel Bible College in Topeka had arrived at this doctrine during the closing days of 1900 and had experienced a dramatic outpouring of the Holy Spirit during which virtually everyone present spoke in tongues. Parham considered this to be a sign of the last days—God's way of restoring to the church apostolic faith of the New Testament. It also confirmed to him that the baptism in the Holy Spirit would be accompanied, or "evidenced," by speaking in tongues.

Parham found many receptive souls in Houston, including Seymour's friend Lucy Farrow, who heartily welcomed his message. Farrow developed such a friendship with the Parhams that they invited her to serve as a governess to their children when they returned to their home in Baxter Springs. She turned the pastorate of her congregation over to Seymour and, while staying

**REVIVAL IN HOUSTON**
*In summer 1905, Parham (seated in the center of the third row) conducted a citywide crusade in Houston's Bryan Hall. Many there embraced his teaching about the baptism in the Holy Spirit.*

in the Parham home in Baxter Springs, Kansas, experienced her own Spirit baptism and spoke in tongues.

In fall 1905 Farrow returned with the Parhams to Houston for another crusade at Bryan Hall. Parham was now planning to open a Bible school on January 1, 1906, and Farrow encouraged Seymour to enroll. Seymour, still driven by a deep desire for God, immediately applied for admission, but his application posed a problem because of Jim Crow laws and customs that mandated racial segregation. Parham skirted these rules by allowing Seymour to sit in an adjoining room and listen to classes

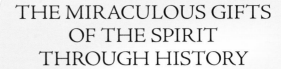

# THE MIRACULOUS GIFTS OF THE SPIRIT THROUGH HISTORY

The work of the Holy Spirit and His gifts, including speaking in tongues, have occurred among Christians for the past two thousand years and were especially common during the first three centuries of the church's existence. Irenaeus, the well-known church father of the second century, spoke of healings, exorcisms, and even the raising of the dead in his time. He also said, "In like manner we do also hear many brethren in the church who possess prophetic gifts and who through the Spirit speak all kinds of languages." In the third century, the African church father Tertullian spoke of prophetic gifts and gifts of healing. He challenged the teachings of the heretic Marcion with logical arguments and then challenged him to prove his validity by demonstrating that miraculous gifts were operative in his life. He said, "Let him produce a psalm, a vision, a prayer—only let it be by the Spirit, in an ecstasy, that is in a rapture whenever an interpretation of tongues has occurred. *Now all these signs are forthcoming from my side without any difficulty.*"[2]

In the United States there were movings of the Holy Spirit as early as 1854 in New England among those who were known as "the Gift People." At Moorhead, Minnesota, in 1903, under the ministry of John Thompson, a minister of the Swedish Mission, the Holy Spirit was outpoured, and those receiving the Spirit spoke in new tongues.... The Holy Spirit was outpoured in the early days of [the Church of God] at the Shearer Schoolhouse in Cherokee County, North Carolina, and those who were baptized in the Holy Spirit spoke in tongues, others prophesied, and miracles of healing occurred.[3]

## FROM *THE APOSTOLIC FAITH,* OCTOBER 1906 ISSUE

### THE APOSTOLIC FAITH

"Earnestly contend for the faith which was once delivered unto the saints."—Jude 3.

Vol. 1, No. 2     Los Angeles, Cal. October, 1906     Subscription Free

#### The Pentecostal Baptism Restored

**The Promised Latter Rain Now Being Poured Out on God's Humble People.**

Five years ago, God put it into [Charles Parham's] heart to go over to To-peka, Kansas, to educate missionaries to carry the Gospel. It was a faith school, and the Bible was the only textbook. The students had gathered there without tuition or board, God sending in the means to carry on the work. . . . Parham became convinced that there was no religious school that tallied up with the second chapter of Acts. Just before the first of January, 1901, the Bible School began to study the Word on the Baptism with the Holy Ghost to discover the Bible evidence of this baptism that they might obtain it.

The students kept up continual prayer in the praying tower. A company would go up and stay three hours, and then another company would go up and wait on God, praying that all the promises of the Word might be wrought out in their lives.

On New Year's night, Miss Agnes N. Ozman was convinced of the need of a personal Pentecost. A few minutes before midnight, she desired hands laid on her that she might receive the gift of the Holy Ghost. During prayer and invocation of hands, she was filled with the Holy Ghost and spoke with other tongues as the Spirit gave utterance.

This made all hungry. Scarcely eating or sleeping, the school with one accord waited on God. On the 3rd of January, 1901, suddenly twelve students were filled with the Holy Ghost and began to speak with other tongues, and when Bro. Parham returned and opened the door of the room where they were gathered, a wonderful sight met his eyes. The whole room was filled with a white sheen of light that could not be described, and twelve of the students were on their feet talking in different languages.

He said they seemed to pay no attention at all to him, and he knelt in one corner and said: "O God, what does this mean?" The Lord said: "Are you able to stand for the experience in the face of persecution and howling mobs?" He said: "Yes, Lord, if You will give me the experience, for the laborer must first be partaker of the fruits." Instantly the Lord took his vocal organs, and he was preaching the Word in another language.[4]

**OUTPOURING**
*Agnes N. Ozman, pictured in 1937, was the first person to speak in tongues at Parham's Bethel Bible College in 1901.*

---

through an open door. There, Seymour imbibed Parham's teaching of a baptism in the Holy Spirit evidenced by speaking in tongues.

## THE INVITATION TO LOS ANGELES

While attending classes and continuing to pastor his congregation in Houston, Seymour was invited to pastor a Los Angeles storefront Holiness mission whose parishioners were mostly black. This group had been expelled from the Second Baptist Church in Los Angeles because they had accepted the holiness teaching of a second blessing of sanctification. One of their members, Neeley Terry, had attended Seymour's church in Houston and was favorably impressed with him. She returned to Los Angeles, and her church promptly invited Seymour to pastor

**RAISING THE BANNER**
*Parham (front) and followers outside a courthouse at Carthage, Missouri (c. 1905).*

their congregation. After prayerfully considering the offer, Seymour accepted it and departed Houston in February 1906.

Seymour had not received the baptism in the Holy Spirit, but he was prepared to preach it without compromise. In his first service at the mission in Los Angeles he broached the subject of this so-called third blessing, but his audience equated the baptism in the Holy Spirit with their experience of sanctification and rejected the idea that tongues was necessary. When Seymour returned for the evening service, he found the door padlocked. The elders had decided he was preaching false doctrine. Less than a week after arriving in Los Angeles, Seymour was without a church.

**EARLY FOLLOWERS**
*Parham and others in front of an Apostolic Faith mission, possibly at Joplin, Missouri (c. 1910). Their flag reads, "Our God, the Healer of His People."*

*"It was the divine call that brought me from Houston, Texas, to Los Angeles."*

**BURGEONING MOVEMENT**
*A camp meeting at Brunner Tabernacle in Houston, Texas (c. 1906). Parham is in the second row by the post and Howard Goss is in the front row on the far right. The sign reads, "Apostolic faith. Our faith is built on experiential salvation."*

*In His Own Words*

## WILLIAM SEYMOUR'S CALL TO LOS ANGELES

*It was the divine call that brought me from Houston, Texas, to Los Angeles. The Lord put it in the heart of one of the saints in Los Angeles to write to me that she felt the Lord would have me come over here and do a work, and I came, for I felt it was the leading of the Lord. The Lord sent the means, and I came to take charge of a mission on Santa Fe Street, and one night they locked the door against me, and afterwards got Bro. Roberts, the president of the Holiness Association, to come down and settle the doctrine of the Baptism with the Holy Ghost, that it was simply sanctification. He came down and a good many holiness preachers with him, and they stated that sanctification was the baptism with the Holy Ghost. But yet they did not have the evidence at the second chapter of Acts, for when the disciples were all filled with the Holy Ghost, they spoke in tongues as the Spirit gave utterance. After the president heard me speak of what the true baptism of the Holy Ghost was, he said he wanted it too, and told me that when I had received it to let him know. So I received it and let him know. The beginning of the Pentecost started in a cottage prayer meeting at 214 Bonnie Brae.[5]*

# REVIVAL BREAKS
FORTH

# REVIVAL BREAKS FORTH

Some members of the mission took compassion on Seymour and invited him to stay in the homes of Edward Lee and then Richard Asberry, who lived at 214 Bonnie Brae Street. Seymour, driven by an almost overwhelming hunger for the power of the Holy Spirit, spent nearly all his time in prayer. He later said:

> I got to Los Angeles, and there the hunger [to have more of God] was not less but more. I prayed, "God, what can I do?" The Spirit said, "Pray more." "But Lord, I am praying five hours a day now." I increased my hours of prayer to seven, and prayed on.... I prayed to God to give what Parham preached, the real Holy Ghost and fire with tongues with love and power of God like the apostles had.[6]

Because of Seymour's devotion to prayer, the Asberrys opened their home to evening prayer meetings. Seymour told the group about Lucy Farrow, who had introduced him to the idea of the baptism in the Holy Spirit. They were so anxious to meet her that they took up an offering for her train fare and invited her to come.

A few days later Edward Lee returned home after work to find Farrow just arrived from Houston. He was so hungry for the baptism in the Holy Spirit that after a brief introduction he implored, "Sister, if you will lay your hands on me, I believe I will get my baptism right now." She replied, "I cannot do it unless the Lord says so." Later, while eating dinner, Farrow rose from her seat, walked over to Lee, and said, "The Lord tells me to lay my hands on you for the Holy Ghost." She laid her hands on Lee, who immediately fell out of his chair and, while lying on the floor, began speaking in tongues.[7]

**BEGINNINGS**
*At left, William J. Seymour with wife, Jennie Moore Seymour (1912). Below, the house on Bonnie Brae Street (1976) where Seymour's prayer meeting blossomed into the Azusa Street revival.*

All photos courtesy of *Flower Pentecostal Heritage Center*

*"As the people came in they would fall under God's power; and the whole city was stirred. They shouted there until the foundation of the house gave way."*

**A NEW SONG**
*When revival broke out at the Bonne Brae Street home of Richard and Ruth Asberry (top) on April 9, 1906, Jennie Seymour, pictured in 1907, played the piano and sang in the Spirit, never having had a lesson.*

## REVIVAL COMES

Later that day the Lees and Farrow went to the Asberry home for the evening prayer meeting. Edward Lee walked through the door, lifted his hands, and broke out in tongues. Suddenly the power of God flooded the room, and virtually everyone present began speaking in tongues. One of those present was Jennie Moore, who later became Seymour's wife. She not only spoke in tongues but also went to the piano and played and sang in tongues, though she had never had a lesson.[8] An eyewitness to these events said:

They shouted three days and three nights. It was the Easter season. The people came from everywhere. By the next morning there was no way of getting near the house. As the people came in they would fall under God's power; and the whole city was stirred. They shouted there until the foundation of the house gave way, but no one was hurt. During those three days there were many people who received their baptism. The sick were healed and sinners were saved just as they came in.[9]

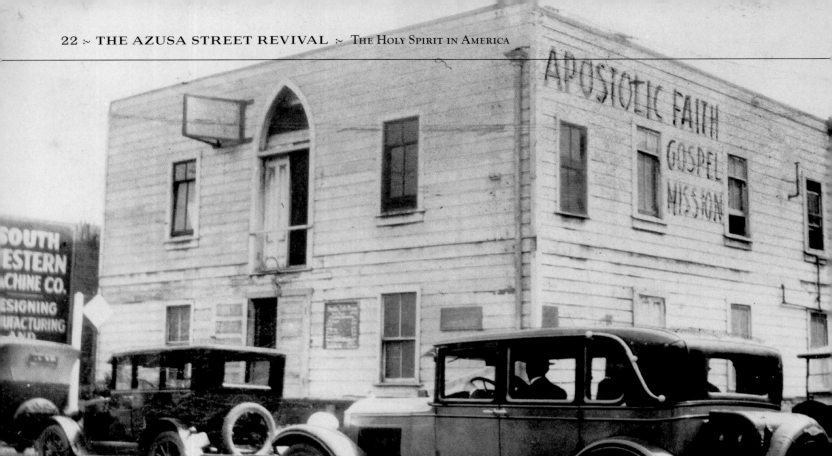

Realizing that the Asberry home was too small to contain the crowds, Seymour and others looked for larger facilities and finally located an older building at 312 Azusa Street in downtown Los Angeles. This two-story structure, measuring 40 feet by 60 feet, had once been a Methodist Episcopal church, but more recently had been used as a stable and warehouse. They removed the debris and installed rough plank benches and a makeshift pulpit made from wooden shoeboxes. On April 14, 1906, they held their first meeting in the new facilities. So began the twentieth century's most momentous revival.

### MOVE TO AZUSA

*The prayer meeting at Bonnie Brae outgrew the Asberry home and was moved to a building on Azusa Street that had recently been used as a stable and warehouse (top, c. 1928). Participants in the Azusa Street Mission, pictured in 1907, included, seated (l-r), Sister Evans, Hiram W. Smith, William Seymour, Clara Lum; standing (l-r), an unidentified woman, Brother Evans (reportedly the first man to receive the baptism in the Holy Spirit at Azusa Street), Jennie Moore (later Mrs. William Seymour), Glenn A. Cook, Florence Crawford, an unidentified man, and Sister Prince. Florence Crawford's daughter Mildred is seated in Hiram Smith's lap.*

# A DAY AT THE AZUSA STREET REVIVAL

The services at Azusa were spontaneous, with no preannounced events, special choirs, singers, or well-known evangelists. There wasn't even a platform. Seymour, the recognized leader, spent much of his time behind the pulpit with his head inside the top shoebox, praying. A contemporary, John G. Lake, described Seymour like so:

> God had put such a hunger into that man's heart that when the fire of God came it glorified him. I do not believe any other man in modern times had a more wonderful deluge of God in his life than God gave to that dear fellow, and the glory and power of a real Pentecost swept the world. That black man preached to my congregation of ten thousand people when the glory and power of God was upon his spirit, and men shook and trembled and cried to God. God was in him.[10]

Prayer consumed the participants at Azusa Street. One participant said, "The whole place was steeped in prayer."[11] During meetings anyone was free to share a testimony or word of exhortation. One participant described a typical service.

> Someone might be speaking. Suddenly the Spirit would fall upon the congregation. God Himself would give the altar call. Men

---

# THE APOSTOLIC

"Earnestly contend for the faith which was once delivered unto the saints."

Vol. 1, No. 2
Los Angeles, Cal., 1906

**The first issue of Seymour's newspaper, *The Apostolic Faith*, was published in September 1906. The lead story read:**

## PENTECOST HAS COME

*Los Angeles Being Visited by a Revival of Bible Salvation and Pentecost as Recorded in the Books of Acts*

The power of God now has this city agitated as never before. Pentecost has surely come and with it the Bible evidences are following, many being converted and sanctified and filled with the Holy Ghost, speaking in tongues as they did on the day of Pentecost. The scenes that are daily enacted in the building on Azusa street and at Missions and churches in other parts of the city are beyond description, and the real revival is only started, as God has been working with His children mostly, getting them through to Pentecost, and laying the foundation for a mighty wave of salvation among the unconverted.

The meetings are held in an old Methodist church that had been converted in part into a tenement house, leaving a large, unplastered, barn-like room on the ground floor. Here about a dozen congregated each day, holding meetings on Bonnie Brae in the evening.... In a short time God began to manifest His power and soon the building could not contain the people. Now the meetings continue all day and into the night and the fire is kindling all over the city and surrounding towns. Proud, well-dressed preachers come in to "investigate." Soon their high looks are replaced with wonder, then conviction comes, and very often you will find them in a short time wallowing on the dirty floor, asking God to forgive them and make them as little children.

It would be impossible to state how many have been converted, sanctified and filled with the Holy Ghost. They have been and are daily going out to all points of the compass to spread this wonderful gospel.[12]

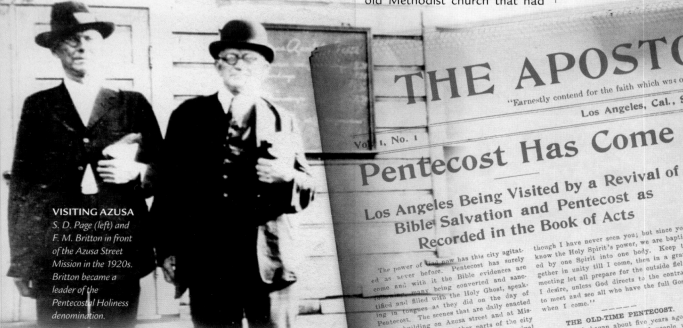

**VISITING AZUSA**
*S. D. Page (left) and F. M. Britton in front of the Azusa Street Mission in the 1920s. Britton became a leader of the Pentecostal Holiness denomination.*

## THE APOSTOLIC F

"Earnestly contend for the faith which was once delivered unto the saints."—Jude

Los Angeles, Cal., September, 1906

Vol 1, No. 1

### Pentecost Has Come

Los Angeles Being Visited by a Revival of Bible Salvation and Pentecost as Recorded in the Book of Acts

The Lord has given the gift of writing in unknown languages, also the gift of playing on instruments.

A little girl who walked with crutches and had tuberculosis of the bones, as the doctor declared, was healed and dropped her crutches and began to skip about the yard.

All over this city, God has been saving homes on fire and coming down and saving and sanctifying and baptizing with the Holy Ghost.

Many churches have been praying for Pentecost, and Pentecost has come. The question now, will they accept it? God is here now, will they accept it? God is here now, will they accept it?

The secular papers have been stirred and published reports against the movement, which has only resulted in drawing hungry souls who understand that where the devil fights a thing unless God was in it, they have come and found it was indeed of God.

The power of God now has this city agitated as never before. Pentecost has surely come and with it the Bible evidences are following, many being converted and sanctified and filled with the Holy Ghost, speaking as they did on the day of Pentecost. The scenes that are daily enacted in the building on Azusa street and at Missions and churches in other parts of the city are beyond description, and the real revival is only started, as God has been working with

though I have never seen you; but since you know the Holy Spirit's power, we are baptized by one Spirit into one body. Keep together in unity till I come, then in a grand meeting let all prepare for the outside fields. I desire, unless God directs to the contrary, to meet and see all who have the full Gospel when I come.

### THE OLD-TIME PENTECOST.

This work began about five years ago last January, when a company of people under the leadership of Chas. Parham, who were seeking God's word, tarried for Pentecost, praying and searching through the

# REVIVAL MAKES FRONT PAGE NEWS

*On April 18, just four days after moving into the Azusa Street location, the revival made the front page of the* Los Angeles Times.

## THE HAPPENINGS AT AZUSA STREET

*Weird Babel of Tongues*

*New Sect of Fanatics Is Breaking Loose*

*Wild Scene Last Night on Azusa Street*

*Gurgle of Wordless Talk by a Sister*

Breathing strange utterances and mouthing a creed which it would seem no sane mortal could understand, the newest religious sect has started in Los Angeles. Meetings are held in a tumbledown shack on Azusa Street, near San Pedro Street, and devotees of the weird doctrine practice the most fanatical rites, preach the wildest theories and work themselves into a state of mad excitement in their peculiar zeal. Colored people and a sprinkling of whites compose the congregation, and night is made hideous in the neighborhood by the howlings of the worshippers who spend hours swaying forth and back in a nerve-racking [sic] attitude of prayer and supplication. They claim to have "the gift of tongues;" and to be able to comprehend the babel.

Such a startling claim has never yet been made by any company of fanatics, even in Los Angeles, the home of almost numberless creeds. Sacred tenets, reverently mentioned by the orthodox believer, are dealt with in a familiar, if not irreverent, manner by these latest religionists.

## STONY OPTIC DEFIES

An old colored exhorter, blind in one eye, is the major-domo of the company. With his stony optic fixed on some luckless unbeliever, the old man yells his defiance and challenges an answer. Anathemas are heaped upon him who shall dare to gainsay the utterances of the preacher.

Clasped in his big fist the colored brother holds a miniature Bible from which he reads at intervals one or two words—never more. After an hour spent in exhortation the brethren present are invited to join in a "meeting of prayer, song and testimony." Then it is that pandemonium breaks loose, and the bounds of reason are passed by those who are "filled with the spirit," whatever that may be.

"You-oo-oo gou-loo-loo come under the bloo-oo-oo boo-loo;" shouts an old colored "mammy;" in a frenzy of religious zeal. Swinging her arms wildly about her, she continues with the strangest harangue ever uttered. Few of her words are intelligible, and for the most part her testimony contains the most outrageous jumble of syllables, which are listened to with awe by the company.

## LET TONGUES COME FORTH

One of the wildest of the meetings was held last night, and the highest pitch of excitement was reached by the gathering, which continued to "worship" until nearly midnight. The old exhorter urged the "sisters" to let the "tongues come forth" and the women gave themselves over to a riot of religious fervor. As a result a buxom dame was overcome with excitement and almost fainted.

Undismayed by the fearful attitude of the colored worshipper, another black women [sic] jumped to the floor and began a wild gesticulation, which ended in a gurgle of wordless prayers which were nothing less than shocking.

"She's speaking in unknown tongues;" announced the leader, in ah [sic] awed whisper, "keep on sister." The sister continued until it was necessary to assist her to a seat because of her bodily fatigue.

## GOLD AMONG THEM

Among the "believers" is a man who claims to be a Jewish rabbi. He says his name is Gold, and claims to have held positions in some of the largest synagogues in the United States. He told the motley company last night that he is well known to the Jewish people of Los Angeles and San Francisco, and referred to prominent local citizens by name. Gold claims to have been miraculously healed and is a convert of the new sect.

Another speaker had a vision in which he saw the people of Los Angeles flocking in a mighty stream to perdition. He prophesied awful destruction to this city unless its citizens are brought to a belief in the tenets of the new faith.[13]

**MOCKED**
*In July 1906, the* Los Angeles Times *printed cartoon caricatures of Pentecostals, showing a man at a pulpit and other scenes.*

tember 18, the *Times* asked Dr. Keyes to "reduce the strange 'language' that suddenly descended upon him to writing."

timately Elmer Fisher established the per Room Misson at 327½ South S

would fall all over the house, like the slain in battle, or rush for the altar *en masse* to seek God. Presumptuous men would sometimes come among us. Especially preachers who would try to spread themselves in self-opinionation. But their effort was short lived. Their minds would wander, their brains reel. Things would turn black before their eyes. They could not go on. We simply prayed. The Holy Ghost did the rest.[14]

The building was never empty of people at prayer, though services, such as they were, usually began spontaneously around mid-morning and continued until three or four the following morning. Dramatic spiritual manifestations captured the attention of the general public, but participants believed the most important feature of the revival was God's love in action. Frank Bartleman, a journalist and participant in the revival, described it as a return to the "first love" of the early church.

Divine love was wonderfully manifest in the meetings. They would not even allow an unkind word said against any of their opposers, or the churches. The message was the love of God. It was a sort of "first love" of the early church returned. The "baptism" as we received it in the beginning did not allow us to think, speak, or hear evil of any man. We knew the moment we had grieved the Spirit by an unkind thought or word. We seemed to live in a sea of pure divine love.[15]

**AZUSA LEADERS**
*Azusa Street revival leaders (c. 1907) in front of the mission. Back row (l-r): Brother Adams, F. F. Bosworth, Tom Hezmalhalch. Seated: William J. Seymour, and John G. Lake.*

## GRACIOUS PENTECOSTAL SHOWERS CONTINUE TO FALL

The news has spread far and wide that Los Angeles is being visited with a "rushing mighty wind from heaven." The how and why of it is to be found in the very opposite of those conditions that are usually thought necessary for a big revival. No instruments of music are used, none are needed. No choir—but bands of angels have been heard by some in the spirit and there is a heavenly singing that is inspired by the Holy Ghost. No collections are taken. No bills have been posted to advertise the meetings. No church or organization is back of it. All who are in touch with God realize as soon as they enter the meetings that the Holy Ghost is the leader. One brother stated that even before his train entered the city, he felt the power of the revival.[16]

*"We knew the moment we had grieved the Spirit by an unkind thought or word. We seemed to live in a sea of pure divine love."*

# FRANK BARTLEMAN

Frank Bartleman, an early Pentecostal evangelist and journalist, became the primary chronicler of the Azusa Street revival. Bartleman, known as something of a loner, participated in meetings at Azusa Street from 1906 to 1908 and wrote articles about the revival for various Christian publications. After departing Los Angeles, Bartleman preached throughout the United States and made an around-the-world ministry tour. He published his eyewitness of account of the Azusa Street revival in 1925 under the title *How Pentecost Came to Los Angeles*. The book is currently published under the title *Azusa Street*. Bartleman died in Burbank, California, in 1936.[17]

## CROWDS FROM AROUND THE WORLD

At first the revival advanced slowly, with only 150 people receiving "the gift of the Holy Ghost and the Bible evidence" during the summer of 1906. But this changed in the fall as the revival gained momentum.[18] News of the revival began to raise wide interest, and soon the faithful and curious journeyed from far and near to experience it. Though passage was long and difficult, visitors poured in from across North America and from foreign soil, where word had spread among missionaries. The *Los Angeles Times'* negative coverage nevertheless caught people's attention. Bartleman sent his articles about the revival to Holiness publications throughout the country. Seymour founded a paper called *The Apostolic Faith*, which eventually reached a distribution of 40,000 copies. For practical purposes the prayer meeting was soon organized into a church called the Apostolic Faith Mission.

Many visitors had dramatic spiritual experiences unlike anything they had ever known before. Visitor Glenn A. Cook shared his testimony with *The Apostolic Faith* newspaper:

I could feel the power going through me like electric needles. The Spirit taught me that I must not resist the power but give way and become limp as a piece of cloth. When I did this, I fell under the power, and God began to mold me and teach me what it meant to be really surrendered to Him. I was laid out under the power five times before Pentecost really came. Each time I would come out from under the power, I would feel so sweet and clean, as though I had been run through a washing machine.... My arms began to tremble, and soon I was shaken violently by a great power, and it seemed as though a large pipe was fitted over my neck, my head apparently being off.... About thirty hours afterwards, while sitting in the meeting on Azusa Street, I felt my throat and tongue begin to move, without any effort on my part. Soon I began to stutter and then out came a distinct language which I could hardly restrain. I talked and laughed with joy far into the night.[19]

Another visitor, G. W. Batman wrote, "I received the baptism with the Holy Ghost and

**REVIVAL'S JOURNALIST**
*Frank Bartleman (left, c. 1894) as a young man, and pictured at 8th and Maple Street Pentecostal Assembly in Los Angeles, where he ministered.*

fire and now I feel the presence of the Holy Ghost, not only in my heart but in my lungs, my hands, my arms and all through my body and at times I am shaken like a locomotive steamed up and prepared for a long journey."[20]

Countless thousands had similar deeply personal experiences, spoke in tongues, wept, and went home with fresh zeal and empowerment to spread the gospel.

## CHRIST AT THE CENTER OF AZUSA STREET

Though Azusa Street quickly became known for the manifestations of the Holy Spirit, like miraculous gifts and speaking in tongues, the participants kept their attention squarely on Jesus. Frank Bartleman expressed the general desire that Jesus should not be "lost in the temple" by the exaltation of the Holy Ghost and of the gifts of the Spirit. "I endeavored to keep Him as the central theme and figure before the people," Bartleman said. "The Holy Ghost never draws attention from Christ to Himself, but rather reveals Christ in a fuller way." When once asked by a certain woman to pray that she might speak in tongues, Seymour kindly exhorted, "Now, look here, Sister Sadie, don't you ever go looking for tongues. Seek Jesus for Himself. Seek the Lord. He's the One."

### In Their Own Words...

*The Holy Spirit fell upon me and filled me literally, as it seemed to lift me up, for indeed, I was in the air in an instant, shouting, 'Praise God,' and instantly I began to speak in another language. I could not have been more surprised if at the same moment someone had handed me a million dollars.*[21]

—Account from a Baptist pastor visiting the Azusa Street revival

❖

*By the time the chorus ended, the power of God was so heavy upon me. I could scarcely open my mouth, and every fibre of my being was trembling. Yet my feet felt glued to the floor and my knees stiff, so I could not sit down. I only got out a few broken sentences that I remember. (I never fainted in my life and was never unconscious, but God certainly took me out of myself.) He showed me things which there are not words enough in the English language to express...I was under the power the remainder of the meeting, and for three days was as one drunken...Since then, such waves of power roll over me from time to time. I can scarcely keep my feet, and I am sure if my old friends in California could see me, they would think I was indeed insane.*[22]

—Testimony of Myrtle K. Shideler

❖

*Scenes transpiring here [on Azusa Street] are what Los Angeles churches have been praying for for years. I have been a Methodist for twenty-five years. I was leader of the praying band for the First Methodist Church. We prayed that Pentecost might come to the city of Los Angeles. We wanted it to start in the First Methodist Church, but God did not start it there. I bless God that it did not start in any church in this city, but in a barn, so that we might all come and take part in it. If it had started in a fine church, the poor colored people and Spanish people would not have got it, but praise God it started here.*[23]

—Testimony of a leading Methodist layman of Los Angeles

**TENT MEETING**
*John G. Lake and others on the platform of a revival meeting in Milwaukee, Wisconsin.*

**HIGHWAYS AND BYWAYS**

*An evangelistic team and house trailer at Hickory Grove, Oklahoma, in 1912.*

# DENOMINATIONS SWEPT INTO REVIVAL

# DENOMINATIONS SWEPT INTO REVIVAL

Photo courtesy of IPHC

I N NOVEMBER 1906, GASTON B. CASHWELL, AN EVAN-
GELIST WITH THE PENTECOSTAL HOLINESS CHURCH
OF NORTH CAROLINA, ARRIVED AT THE AZUSA STREET
MISSION. HE HAD READ OF THE REVIVAL IN A PUBLICATION
CALLED THE *WAY OF FAITH* AND HAD COME TO SEE FOR HIM-
SELF IF AZUSA STREET WAS THE REVIVAL HE AND OTHERS
HAD BEEN PRAYING FOR. SO DESPERATE WAS CASHWELL FOR
A DEEPER WALK WITH GOD THAT HE BORROWED MONEY FOR
A ONE-WAY TRAIN TICKET AND, WEARING HIS ONLY SUIT,
CAME TO LOS ANGELES.

During Cashwell's first service at the Azusa Street Mission, a young black man laid his hands on him and prayed that he might receive the "baptism." Such close racial interaction rankled Cashwell, and he left the meeting offended and disappointed. Back in his hotel

### ON THE EAST COAST, "ANOTHER AZUSA STREET"

After returning home to Dunn, North Carolina, Cashwell preached in the local Holiness church and told of his experience in Los Angeles. Interest ran so high that he

**REVIVAL SPREADS EAST**
*G. B. Cashwell (above) visited the Azusa Street revival, then led a powerful revival in North Carolina that transformed many lives and several denominations in the South and East.*

> Thousands crowded into the warehouse, and scores were baptized in the Holy Spirit and spoke in tongues.

room he "suffered a crucifixion" as God dealt severely with him about his racial prejudice. He later said that God gave him a love for blacks and a renewed hunger to be baptized in the Holy Spirit. He returned to the mission the next night and asked Seymour and several young black people to lay their hands on him and pray that he might receive the baptism in the Holy Spirit. Cashwell received his Spirit baptism and, according to his own account, spoke in English, German, and French.[24] Seymour received an offering for him and presented him with a new suit and enough money for his return fare to North Carolina.

rented a three-story tobacco warehouse and conducted a month-long Pentecostal revival. Thousands crowded into the warehouse, and scores were baptized in the Holy Spirit and spoke in tongues. People came from all over the Southeast, and the revival became for the East Coast "another Azusa Street."[25]

Among the attendees were pastors and leaders from the four largest Holiness groups in the area: the Pentecostal Holiness churches, the Fire-Baptized Holiness churches, Holiness Free-Will Baptist churches, and Tabernacle Pentecostal churches. Many of these pastors were baptized in the Holy Spirit and spoke

All photos (except noted) courtesy of *Flower Pentecostal Heritage Center*

# REVIVAL IN ZION CITY, ILLINOIS

Zion City, Illinois, forty miles north of Chicago on Lake Michigan, was founded as a Christian city by well-known healing revivalist John Alexander Dowie. Many devout Christians relocated to Zion from across the United States and from other nations. Their dream of living in a Christian utopia was shattered, however, when the city was plunged into bankruptcy and Dowie was ousted from leadership. Into this tumultuous atmosphere Charles Parham arrived in 1906 with his message of a baptism in the Holy Spirit evidenced by speaking in tongues. Wilbur Voliva, who had just wrested control of the city from Dowie, sought to block Parham's

ministry in Zion by renting every auditorium in the city. Parham responded by conducting meetings in some of the largest homes, including the home of F. F. Bosworth.

A Pentecostal revival erupted, and people crowded into the homes and overflowed onto the lawns. The *Daily Sun* of Waukegan, Illinois, reported that thousands attended the meetings. The work of the Holy Spirit was deep and powerful, according to eyewitness accounts. Many prominent leaders came out of the Zion revival including John G. Lake, F. F. Bosworth, and approximately five hundred other missionaries and ministers.[26]

**MAKING NEWS**
*A Los Angeles newspaper reported December 4, 1906, that a Nebraska woman had received the "gift of tongues."*

in tongues. Almost overnight, these pastors and their churches became full-fledged participants in the Pentecostal revival. The Pentecostal Holiness Church later merged with the Fire-Baptized Holiness Church and the new group retained the name Pentecostal Holiness Church. This group then merged with the Tabernacle Pentecostal Church to form what is today known as the International Pentecostal Holiness Church, one of the oldest and largest Pentecostal denominations.

**ZION CITY'S REVIVAL**
*After Zion City collapsed financially and spiritually under the leadership of John Alexander Dowie, shown (right) wearing high priestly robes as the self-proclaimed first apostle in the Christian Catholic Apostolic Church (1904), the community experienced Pentecostal revival in 1906 under Charles Parham. Pictured above (c. 1909) are participants in that revival.*

# THE CHURCH OF GOD IN CHRIST

Charles H. Mason and the Church of God in Christ (COGIC) were swept into the Pentecostal revival when Mason visited the Azusa Street Mission during the fall of 1906. Mason and Charles Price Jones had founded the Church of God in Christ in 1897 after being ostracized by their Baptist colleagues when they embraced the Wesleyan-Holiness doctrine of sanctification. By 1906 the COGIC had grown into a small network of churches in the South and Southwest.

Mason spent five weeks in Los Angeles, mostly at the Azusa Street Mission praying and seeking the baptism in the Holy Spirit. One day while sitting in the mission, someone said, "Let us sing." Mason stood to his feet and began to sing, "He Brought Me Out of the Miry Clay." He later described what happened.

"The Spirit came upon the saints and upon me. Then I gave up for the Lord to have His way within me. So there came a wave of

**FOUNDER**

*Charles H. Mason cofounded the Church of God in Christ in 1897 and embraced the Pentecostal message in 1906 after visiting the Azusa Street revival. Below, Mason is pictured sitting (front, center) at a COGIC meeting in Memphis, Tennessee, in 1932.*

Glory into me and all of my being was filled with the Glory of the Lord. So when He had gotten me straight on my feet, there came a light which enveloped my entire being above the brightness of the sun. When I opened my mouth to say Glory, a flame touched my tongue which ran down me. My language changed and no word could I speak in my own tongue. Oh! I was filled with the Glory of the Lord. My soul was then satisfied."[27]

When he returned home to Memphis and shared his experience with Jones and their congregation, Mason encountered much opposition. After several days of intense debate, he and Jones separated and the church split. Those who followed Mason reorganized their group and retained the name of Church of God in Christ. The Church of God in Christ, whose constituency is primarily African American, would become the largest Pentecostal denomination in America with a membership estimated at 5.5 million.

# TONGUES AS REAL LANGUAGES

Albert Norton, missionary to India when the Holy Spirit was poured out in 1906, described his amazement at hearing illiterate Indians speaking in fluent English when they were baptized in the Holy Spirit. The following incident occurred in a home for girls operated by Pandita Ramabai, who has been called the "Mother of the Pentecostal Movement" in India.

*One week ago I visited the Mukti Mission. Miss Abrams asked me if I would like to go into a room where about twenty girls were praying. After entering, I knelt with closed eyes by a table on one side. Presently I heard someone praying near me in very distinct English. Among the petitions were, "O Lord, open the mouth; O Lord, open the heart; Oh, the blood of Jesus, the blood of Jesus!" I was struck with such astonishment, as I knew there was no one in the room who could speak English, besides Miss Abrams. I opened my eyes and within three feet of me, on her knees with closed eyes and raised hands was a woman I had baptized at Kedgaon in 1899, and whom my wife and I had known intimately since. Her mother tongue was Marathi and she could speak a little Hindustani. But when I heard her speak English idiomatically, distinctly and fluently, I was impressed as I should have been had I seen one, whom I knew to be dead, raised to life. A few other illiterate Marathi women and girls were speaking in English and some were speaking in other languages which none at Kedgaon understood.*[28]

**PENTECOST IN INDIA**
*Pandita Ramabai (center), known as the "Mother of the Pentecostal Movement" in India, with a group of babies at her Mukti Mission.*

## THE MISSIONS EMPHASIS

Seymour and the others at the Azusa Street revival believed God was pouring out His Spirit to empower Christians to evangelize the world just before the return of Christ to the earth. So strongly did this vision permeate their thinking that in the early days they believed speaking in tongues was missionary tongues by which people would evangelize the heathen. Although they eventually backed away from this misconception, they held firmly to their belief that God was pouring out His Spirit for the sake of world evangelism.

This vision impelled many missionaries to depart from the revival for various parts of the world. Lucy Farrow went to Africa; Alfred and Lillian Garr to India; Samuel and Adrella Mead to Africa; Ansel and Etta Post to Egypt; and Louise Condit and Lucy Leatherman to Jerusalem. Each went in faith, trusting God for provision and relying on the Holy Spirit to lead them in their endeavors.

**GOING FORTH**
*Lillian Garr (right), an early Pentecostal missionary to India, with Lillian Denny.*

# THE MISSIONARY CALL

Many future leaders were called to missions and ministry in the wake of Azusa Street.

MARIE BURGESS BROWN (1880-1971), who became a successful pastor in the Assemblies of God, was baptized in the Holy Spirit in the home of F. F. Bosworth in Zion City. She said:

> I remember October 18, 1906, when the Lord baptized me in the Holy Spirit. For six hours He moved upon me in intercessory prayer for various mission fields. First He took me to China. I saw high stone walls and from beyond them heard the Chinese crying for help. Then the Lord took me to India. There I saw the people of different castes, and I wondered and wept. But even

**PASTOR IN NEW YORK CITY**
*Marie Burgess Brown, pictured in 1960, was baptized in the Holy Spirit in the home of F. F. Bosworth at Zion City and founded Glad Tidings Tabernacle in New York City. Glad Tidings became one of the most prominent Pentecostal churches in the nation.*

> as I wept for India's lost, the Lord showed me the continent of Africa. I preached to those people and they were especially responsive. Then in a vision I went to Japan. There I entered an orphanage, and one by one the children came to me.[29]

Brown assumed that God was calling her to one of these nations as a missionary. After this experience, however, she went to New York City and founded Glad Tidings Tabernacle, which became one of the most prominent Pentecostal churches in the nation. Although she never personally visited any of those nations, the church she pastored for more than sixty years, until her death in 1971, eventually sent missionaries to every nation she had seen in the vision.

# REVIVAL IN CHINA

WILLIAM SIMPSON (1869–1961), Christian and Missionary Alliance missionary to China, was baptized in the Holy Spirit in 1912. Shortly thereafter he returned to the United States and affiliated with the newly formed Assemblies of God. China, however, was still much on his heart, and, at a camp meeting in 1918, an amazing miracle occurred that thrust him back to China. He said:

> In a camp meeting the Spirit spoke just as directly to me as He had spoken long ago to Paul: It was in Chinese through a sister who knew not one word of Chinese, and told me to go back to Taochow on the Tibetan border. So I was sent forth by the Holy Spirit, sailing again on February 4, 1918. The

**WILLIAM SIMPSON**
*Missionary William Simpson (pictured left in 1918, and above c. 1934 with his family) participated in a powerful outpouring of the Spirit in China.*

> Lord opened the way until we reached the border, and as soon as we arrived on that mission field the Spirit of God was poured out.... We received letters inviting us here and there, and wherever we went the Spirit was poured out in Pentecostal power.[30]

# A WORLDWIDE PHENOMENON

The revival at Azusa Street continued unabated for about three years (1906–1909) and was a fountainhead of Pentecost for the entire world. For a time, the revival produced amazing racial harmony in a country divided by racist laws and customs. People of many races met there, and an amazing unity prevailed. Blacks, whites, Mexican Americans, and many others knelt together in prayer and waited for their personal Pentecost. Bartleman said, "The color line was washed away in the blood."[31] The original Azusa board of directors, which governed the affairs of the mission and issued ministerial credentials, consisted of seven women and five men. Five of the women were white and two were black. Of the five men, four were white and one, Seymour, was black.

The revival also brought women into positions of leadership they had not achieved in broader society. Women had not yet won the right to vote in U.S. elections and were excluded by most churches from any real leadership positions. Yet women comprised a majority on the Azusa Street Mission's governing board, and many powerful women evangelists, pastors, and missionaries went forth from the revival. Lucy Farrow took her evangelistic endeavors to Los Angeles, Texas, Virginia, New York, and Liberia, West Africa. Florence Crawford served on the governing board of the Azusa Street Mission and later founded the Apostolic Mission of Portland, Oregon. She served as pastor and overseer of this network of churches until her death in 1936. Emma "Mother" Cotton founded and pastored several churches on the West Coast. These and many other women believed their experience of the Spirit fulfilled Joel's prophecy that was quoted by Peter on the Day of Pentecost.

> And it shall come to pass in the last days, says God, that I will pour out of My Spirit on all flesh; your sons and your daughters shall prophesy....And on My menservants and on My maidservants I will pour out My Spirit in those days; and they will prophesy.
> —Acts 2:17, NKJV

Their experience at Azusa Street gave them a strong vision for egalitarian ministry in the last days.

Ultimately, however, doctrinal and racial strife drove participants apart. Many white people left to begin their own churches and missions. By 1914, the Azusa Street Mission

> For a time, the revival produced amazing racial harmony. People of many races met there, and an amazing unity prevailed.

had become a small, local, black congregation.

Seymour continued as the senior pastor until his death on September 28, 1922, in Los Angeles. His wife, the former Jennie Moore, continued as pastor for several years until her health failed. The mission was torn down in 1931 and the property made into a parking lot. Azusa Street's days as a catalyst for worldwide revival were over, but the influence of the revival had just begun.

**MISSION LEADER**
*Florence L. Crawford with son Raymond and daughter Mildred (c. 1910s).*

**MOTHER COTTON**
*Azusa Street revival participant and church planter Emma L. Cotton with husband Henry (c. 1939).*

**WASHED ANEW**
*The baptism of Hannah Wiley in a river near Joplin, Missouri (c. 1910).*

THE FIRST-BORN FROM THE dead, THAT IN ALL THINGS HE MAY BE PREEMINENT

# REVIVAL SPREADS and DIVERSIFIES

A S PILGRIMS TO AZUSA STREET DEPARTED WITH THE LOVE AND POWER OF GOD BURN-ING IN THEIR HEARTS, THE PENTECOSTAL REVIVAL SPREAD AS FAST AS WORD OF MOUTH COULD CARRY IT. PENTECOSTAL CHURCHES SPRUNG UP THROUGHOUT THE COUNTRY, OFTEN IN THE FORM OF SMALL STOREFRONT MISSIONS. OTHER CHURCHES BECAME IN-FLUENTIAL CENTERS OF REVIVAL AND HELPED SPREAD THE FIRE OF PENTECOST THROUGHOUT THE NATION AND THE WORLD. ONE OF THESE CENTERS WAS THE NORTH AVENUE MISSION IN CHICAGO WHOSE PASTOR, WILLIAM DURHAM, VISITED THE AZUSA STREET REVIVAL IN 1907.

## WILLIAM DURHAM AND REVIVAL IN CHICAGO

Durham had joined a Baptist church in Kentucky in 1891 and was converted seven years later in Minnesota where he had a vision of the crucified Christ. He devoted himself completely to God and three years later, in 1901, became the pastor of the North Avenue Mission in Chicago. Upon hearing of the Azusa Street revival, he journeyed there in March 1907 and was baptized in the Holy Spirit and spoke in tongues. At the same

time, Seymour prophesied to him that wherever he preached, the Holy Spirit would fall upon the people.[32]

Durham returned to Chicago with his new experience and message, and as he preached, a powerful revival broke forth in the North Avenue Mission.

### DURHAM'S MINISTRY
*William H. Durham's first camp meeting (above, c. 1909). Durham is standing in center with his hand raised. At left, Durham with Harry Van Loon (left) in the 1910s.*

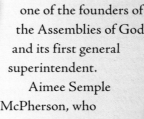

# APOSTOLIC FAITH

*In His Own Words*

**Baptism Restored**

in Now Being Poured Out

William H. Durham recorded his testimony in the sixth issue of *The Apostolic Faith* (February–March 1907), where he wrote:

> On Friday evening, March 1, His mighty power came over me, until I jerked and quaked under it for about three hours. It was strange and wonderful and yet glorious. He worked my whole body, one section at a time, first my arms, then my limbs, then my body, then my head, then my face, then my chin, and finally at 1 a.m. Saturday, March 2, after being under the power for three hours, He finished the work on my vocal organs, and spoke through me in unknown tongues.

WILLIAM H. DURHAM
Fell Asleep in Jesus, July 7th, 1912.

**TESTIMONY**
*The* Pentecostal Testimony *announced William H. Durham's death on its cover in 1912.*

In his periodical the *Pentecostal Testimony*, Durham reported that, "It was nothing to hear people at all hours of the night speaking in tongues and singing in the Spirit."[33] Participants saw a thick haze, like blue smoke, resting upon the mission at times. They said that when this blue haze was present, those entering the mission would fall down in the aisles.[34]

As news of this revival spread, the North Avenue Mission became another important center for Pentecostalism. A. H. Argue of Winnipeg, who became a Pentecostal leader in Canada, received his baptism in the Spirit there, as did E. N. Bell of Texas, who became one of the founders of the Assemblies of God and its first general superintendent.

Aimee Semple McPherson, who later founded the Church of the Foursquare Gospel and became one of America's most famous preachers, visited the revival at North Avenue Mission in 1910 and testified that she was instantly healed of a broken foot during the meeting. She and husband Robert Semple were ordained by Durham and worked with him in evangelistic crusades.

A. H. ARGUE, 1917

E. N. BELL, C. 1920

Seymour and the earliest Pentecostals adopted the name "the Apostolic Faith" for their movement because they believed that God was restoring to the entire church the apostolic faith of the New Testament with accompanying gifts and graces. But eventually those going out from the Los Angeles revival stopped using the term "Apostolic Faith" and instead called themselves "Pentecostals" to put themselves in the same tradition as the disciples on the Day of Pentecost (Acts 2).

## DOCTRINAL CONTROVERSY

In addition to being a catalyst for revival, Durham instigated one of the first major doctrinal controversies of the fledgling movement. Being from a Baptist background, Durham believed sanctification occurred at conversion and was expressed by a growth in grace toward maturity. For him, the baptism in the Holy Spirit was a second blessing. He could not accept the doctrine taught by Seymour and other early Pentecostals of a definite, second work of grace called *sanctification* with the baptism in the Holy Spirit being a third blessing. When he began to openly oppose the Wesleyan-Holiness doctrine of *sanctification*, strife erupted throughout the movement.

Although Durham's teaching on sanctification, which he called "The Finished Work," provoked much dissension throughout the revival, it also had a positive effect. Many hungry souls from non-Wesleyan backgrounds were drawn to Durham's message, and it made it easier for them to embrace the revival. Multitudes reared in Baptist/Reformed churches began embracing the Pentecostal message, further accelerating the movement's astonishing growth. The revival was proving adaptable at drawing people from differing and even opposing theological camps.

# THE CHURCH OF GOD

In the meantime another Holiness denomination based in Cleveland, Tennessee, was drawn into the Pentecostal movement through the ministry of G. B. Cashwell, who became known as "the Apostle of Pentecost to the South." Cashwell visited Cleveland, Tennessee, in 1908 and preached in the local Church of God. This small network of Holiness churches had experienced speaking in tongues at one of their camp meetings in 1898 but had never made tongues an official doctrine of their church. On Sunday, January 12, 1908, A. J. Tomlinson, the general overseer of this denomination, sat on the platform as Cashwell preached on the baptism in the Holy Spirit. As Cashwell spoke, Tomlinson suddenly fell from his chair onto the floor and began speaking in tongues. According to his own testimony, he spoke in ten different languages while lying on the floor. The Church of God instantly became part of the Pentecostal movement and eventually grew to four million adherents worldwide. The denomination sponsored Lee University and the Church of God School of Theology, both in Cleveland, and began operating college-level educational institutions in South Africa, Indonesia, Korea, Puerto Rico, Germany, Panama, Mexico, Argentina, and the Philippines.

**DIVINE SHIFT**
*A. J. Tomlinson, pictured here as a young man, was the general overseer of the Church of God when the denomination embraced the Pentecostal message.*

**PENTECOSTAL Camp Meeting**
To be held at Martinsville, Indiana During the Month of August, 1915

D. V.
...ting will be held at this place
...continuing through-

...during
...cts of a

...ated in a
...essing us.
...Word, and
...rist will be

...shed rooms
...ices.

...Indianapolis
...ce on interur-
...ss:

...er

...tinsville, Indiana

# THE ASSEMBLIES OF GOD

As hundreds of independent Pentecostal churches and missions sprouted up throughout the country, problems and confusion arose along with them. Some churches used the same names without realizing it, most were not legally incorporated, and many independent churches naïvely welcomed anyone claiming to be a Pentecostal preacher. Early Pentecostal leader Howard Goss said, "We soon began hearing from scattered, unpastored churches that they had been invaded by the cleverest of confidence men, posing as our preachers."[35] Strange teachings surfaced, and many Pentecostal preachers with little or no formal education did not know how to address doctrinal aberrations.

Problems also cropped up on the foreign mission field, with some missionaries returning home without establishing a lasting work and others seeming to spend most of their time traveling to and from the field. One Pentecostal periodical expressed the general concern when it declared, "We do feel that some have been sent out who should never have gone."[36] Some leaders began to realize the need for some sort of cooperative fellowship that would quell the problems independent churches could not handle on their own.

Against this background, a call was published in the December issue of the *Word and Witness* for a general council to be convened April 2–12 at the Grand Opera House in Hot Springs, Arkansas. The call was addressed to all Pentecostal churches and assemblies "who desire with united purpose to cooperate in love and peace to push the interests of the kingdom of God everywhere." This call came from the leaders of two groups of Pentecostals, one in Texas and one in Alabama, both known as the Church of God in Christ.

The group in Texas had originally been a part of Parham's Apostolic Faith association. When a part of the group decided to sever ties with Parham in 1907, they went to C. H. Mason of the black Church of God in Christ and requested credentials from his organization

since it was already officially incorporated. This new group then adopted the name Church of God in Christ after the name of Mason's network of churches. Legally, they were a white branch of the black organization but functioned independently of it. E. N. Bell, a seminary-trained Baptist from Fort Worth, rose to prominent leadership of this group and was the editor of their paper, the *Apostolic Faith*.

In 1913 the Texas group merged with a small denomination in Alabama with the same name. The Alabama group was led by M. M. Pinson and H. G. Rodgers, both of whom had been baptized in the Holy Spirit through the ministry of G. B. Cashwell. The new organization retained the name Church of God in Christ and appointed Bell to edit their paper, *Word and Witness*. The leaders of this newly formed Church of God in Christ issued the call for a general council of "Holy Ghost" saints in Hot Springs.

**BIRTHPLACE OF A FELLOWSHIP**
*Pentecostal leaders met at the Grand Opera House in Hot Springs, Arkansas, in 1914. The* Word and Witness *reported on the meetings and declared "God's Glory Present."*

**FIRST GENERAL COUNCIL**
*Attendees of the first General Council of the Assemblies of God. Front row kneeling (l-r): J. W. Welch, M. M. Pinson, T. K. Leonard, J. Roswell Flower, Cyrus Fockler, Howard Goss, E. N. Bell, and Daniel C. O. Opperman.*

*In His Own Words*

## A FUTURE ASSEMBLIES OF GOD OFFICIAL IMPACTED AT AZUSA STREET

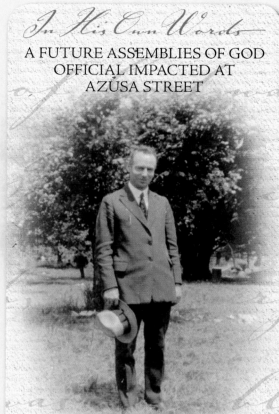

Ernest S. Williams, who later served as general superintendent of the Assemblies of God (1929–1949), visited the Azusa Street revival in 1907 and was astounded by what he encountered:

> *I wish I could describe what I saw. Prayer and worship were everywhere. The altar area was filled with seekers; some were kneeling; others were prone on the floor; some were speaking in tongues. Everyone was doing something; all were seemingly lost in God. I simply stood and looked, for I had never seen anything like it.* [37]

Shortly thereafter, Williams received his own personal Pentecost and spoke in tongues. Much later he said:

> *Soon it will be 59 years since I was filled with the Holy Spirit. I still have my seasons of refreshing from the presence of the Lord, speaking in other tongues and at times shaking under the influence of the Holy Spirit.* [38]

**EXECUTIVE PRESBYTERY**
*The first Executive Presbytery of the Assemblies of God in 1914, at Hot Springs, Arkansas. Front (l-r): T. K. Leonard, E. N. Bell, Cyrus Fockler. Standing in back: John W. Welch, J. Roswell Flower, Daniel C. O. Opperman, Howard A. Goss, M. M. Pinson.*

The convention convened April 2 with more than three hundred in attendance from twenty mostly Midwestern states. About one hundred twenty registered as ministers or missionaries and official delegates. Prominent names in the movement were present: John G. Lake, F. F. Bosworth, J. Roswell Flower, and, of course, Bell, Rodgers, and Pinson. Because many Pentecostals distrusted the idea of organizing, the conveners of this convention set aside the first three days for prayer, worship, and hearing reports and testimonies from those in attendance. This relaxed the tensions and cultivated a sense of unity.

As participants prayed and praised, they felt a distinct sense of God's presence filling the old opera house. One participant recalled a "halo of glory" that rested over the sessions. M. M. Pinson brought the keynote address entitled "The Finished Work of Calvary," which clearly indicated this incipient organization's stance on the controversial subject of sanctification. The Assemblies of God thus represented the formation of the first white, Baptistic/Reformed Pentecostal denomination. The Assemblies of God would become the world's largest denomination with a global constituency of more than fifty million and an American constituency of almost three million.

**ASSEMBLIES OF GOD LEADER**
*F. F. Bosworth and family in the 1920s.*

**PREACHERS OF THE WORD**
*Early Assemblies of God leader Cyrus Fockler (right) with John G. Lake.*

# ONENESS PENTECOSTALS

At a highly publicized Pentecostal camp meeting in Los Angeles in 1913, one of the speakers noted in passing that the record in Acts indicated that the apostles baptized in the name of Jesus Christ rather than in the traditional formula of Father, Son, and Holy Spirit. One of the attendees, intrigued by what he heard, spent the night studying and meditating on the name of Jesus. In the early morning hours he ran through the camp shouting that God had revealed to him the truth of baptism in the name of the Lord Jesus Christ.

One of those attending the camp meeting was Pastor Frank Ewart, who was profoundly impacted by what he heard. He spent the next year quietly studying the issue and then decided it was time to act. He set up a tent in Belvedere, near Los Angeles, and with another Pentecostal evangelist, Glenn Cook, began preaching that baptism was to be in the name of "Jesus only." They also set up a baptismal tank under the tent and baptized each other according to the newly discovered formula. From Los Angeles, the teaching spread rapidly, gaining adherents and stirring heated controversy.

Along with the doctrine of baptism in the name of Jesus Christ, the Oneness Pentecostals developed a parallel theory of the Godhead that says that the terms "Father," "Son," and "Holy Spirit" refer to the same person in differing modes of existence or relationship.

Just as one person in different relationships may be a father, a son, and a brother, so Jesus is Father, Son, and Holy Spirit, they said.

By 1916 the teaching had gained so many adherents that it was the central issue at the 1916 general council of the Assemblies of God. The council voted for a statement of faith that strongly endorsed the historic doctrine of the Trinity and baptism in the name of the Father, Son, and Holy Spirit. As a result, 156 of the 585 ministers left the organization along with the churches they represented.

The Oneness Pentecostals formed the Pentecostal Assemblies of the World, which is primarily black, and the United Pentecostal Church, which is primarily white. Much later, in 1971, the Apostolic World Christian Fellowship was formed to give unity to the many Oneness Pentecostal churches, fellowships, and denominations. The organization grew to represent 3.5 million people.[39]

**NEW DIRECTION**
*A photograph of what is said to be the first Oneness baptismal service east of the Mississippi River, held in Indianapolis, March 6, 1915. Glenn Cook (left) is rebaptizing L. V. Roberts.*

**ONENESS FOUNDERS**
*Frank J. Ewart (right, 1946) and Glenn A. Cook (above, at Murphy Hall in Indianapolis, 1907) began baptizing people in the name of Jesus only, which led to the creation of many Oneness Pentecostal churches and denominations.*

# AIMEE SEMPLE MCPHERSON AND THE INTERNATIONAL CHURCH OF THE FOURSQUARE GOSPEL

The Azusa Street revival indirectly produced one of the century's most fascinating, dynamic, and famous Pentecostal leaders. Aimee Semple McPherson, born Aimee Kennedy in Ingersoll, Ontario, Canada, was ordained by William Durham at the North Avenue Mission in Chicago with first husband Robert. The couple departed as missionaries to China, where Robert soon died of malaria.

Aimee returned to America and married Harold McPherson of Providence, Rhode Island. In June 1916 they launched into an evangelistic

All photos (except noted) courtesy of *Flower Pentecostal Heritage Center*

ministry in churches and auditoriums across America. The grueling lifestyle frayed their marriage, and in 1921 Harold returned to Providence and filed for divorce. The divorce was granted in August of that year.

Aimee continued her ministry and distinguished herself as a powerful and effective preacher. Many said they were miraculously healed through her prayers, and Sister Aimee attracted large crowds as she traveled across the nation. She made the front pages of the newspapers. In Canton the headlines screamed "Cripples Are Cured When Woman

Evangelist Prays." In Denver, twelve thousand people crowded the auditorium every night during her month-long revival crusade there in 1921.

In 1922, while preaching in Oakland, California, Aimee had a vision of Jesus as Savior, baptizer in the Holy Spirit, healer, and coming King. She began to preach what she called "the Foursquare Gospel." Settling in Los Angeles, she built the 5,300-seat Angelus Temple that was dedicated debt-free on January 1, 1923. For three years she preached to capacity crowds every night and three times on Sunday. The following year she became the first woman to be granted a license by the FCC to operate a radio station, KFSG in Los Angeles.

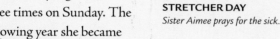

**STRETCHER DAY**
*Sister Aimee prays for the sick.*

Aimee founded Lighthouse of International Foursquare Evangelism (L.I.F.E.) Bible College in 1923, and in 1927 the Church of the Foursquare Gospel was established to facilitate the college's growing network of churches and ministers. Aimee continued as president of the organization until her death in 1944. The International Church of the Foursquare Gospel became one of the fastest growing denominations in the world, with 4 million adherents and 38,000 churches in 141 nations.

**FOURSQUARE BEGINNINGS**
*Revival meeting (below) with Aimee Semple McPherson (right detail) held sometime in the early 1900s. Also pictured is Alice Kersey, grandmother of publisher Stephen Strang (left detail). At right, the front cover of* Bridal Call Foursquare *magazine, August 1927, and a postcard of Angelus Temple from 1924.*

**SONGWRITER**
*Herbert Buffum (immediate right, with family) was one of the leading songwriters of early Pentecost, penning 10,000 songs including the well-known "Lift Me Up Above the Shadows" and "I'm Going Thro', Jesus." Upon his death in 1939, the Los Angeles Times called him the king of gospel songwriters. The Herbert and Lillie Buffum family with Alice Kersey (later Mrs. A. R. Farley) in 1913. The children from left, Naomi, Herbert, Jr., and Ruth. Stephen Strang, founder and publisher of Charisma, is a grandson of Alice Kersey Farley.*
Photo courtesy of *Lorna Medway*

# THE REVIVAL ADAPTS AND SPREADS

Early Pentecostals never intended to establish new denominations, but rather envisioned a mighty revival sweeping the entire church, unifying all believers in the power of the Spirit in preparation for the

every American city of three thousand or more and in every part of the world from Iceland to Tanzania. Pentecostals were already publishing literature in thirty languages.[41] Early Pentecostals saw this as a spontaneous

## The movement grew rapidly and by the 1940s began to capture the attention of the other churches and denominations.

return of Christ to the earth.[40] But by 1914 it was obvious that the revival movement was institutionalizing into denominations, usually defined along racial and doctrinal lines.

In a way, the early divisions in the Pentecostal movement reflected the resilience of the revival and its adaptability to different cultures and doctrinal backgrounds. By 1908, just two years into the revival, the movement had taken root in more than fifty nations. By 1914, Azusa-inspired churches were in

spiritual eruption orchestrated by the Holy Spirit, and it strengthened their conviction that this outpouring of the Holy Spirit would usher in the end of the age and the coming of Christ.

New churches and denominations continued to form, but by 1925 the major racial and doctrinal divides of the movement were in place. The movement grew rapidly and by the 1940s began to capture the attention of the other churches and denominations.

*The Rev. E. M. Adams family at a tent revival at Hanna, Oklahoma, in 1925.*

**PENTECOST SPREADS**

*M.B. Netzel baptizing a woman at Texas City, Texas, in the 1930s as a large crowd watches from a pier.*

# GROWTH AND ACCEPTANCE

# GROWTH AND ACCEPTANCE

**T**HE WORLD DID NOT ALWAYS WELCOME PENTECOSTALS AS THEY SPREAD THEIR SPIRIT-FILLED MESSAGE. EARLY PENTECOSTALS WERE RIDICULED, REJECTED, AND EVEN PHYSICALLY ATTACKED. ONLY FOUR DAYS AFTER THE FIRST SERVICE ON AZUSA STREET, THE *LOS ANGELES TIMES* HEAPED SCORN UPON IT. BARTLEMAN SAID, "THEY WROTE US UP SHAMEFULLY."[42] THIS SORT OF DERISION BECAME TYPICAL OF THE EARLY CLIMATE OF HOSTILITY TOWARD PENTECOSTALS. LOCAL LAW ENFORCEMENT OFTEN TARGETED PREACHERS FOR ARREST, USUALLY FOR DISTURBING THE PEACE OR PRACTICING DIVINE HEALING.

**CRITIC**
*G. Campbell Morgan, the "prince of expositors" and longtime pastor of Westminster Chapel in London, called Pentecostalism "the last vomit of Satan."*

An account in a 1910 issue of the *Church of God Evangel* told of three Pentecostal evangelists who were falsely arrested in the midst of their tent revival in Alabama.

> They marched us out from our tent and up the street to the stone jail. Immediately they left the jail and returned to the tent, cut it down and set fire to it. While the flames were ascending we were in the iron cells praising God that we were counted worthy to suffer shame for His name.[43]

Ruffians and hoodlums tried to intimidate Pentecostals and disrupt their meetings, throwing rotten fruit, eggs, and sometimes stones at the preacher and his audience. Jewell Nicholson Cunningham, whose father was a Pentecostal preacher in the early days of the revival in Oklahoma, remembered the intense opposition they faced in the town of Bixby, just south of Tulsa.

> Men would come right into the service and yell curses louder than Papa could preach.

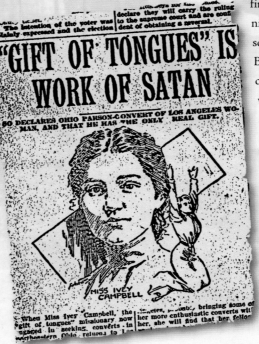

**"GIFT OF TONGUES" IS WORK OF SATAN**

SO DECLARES OHIO PARSON-CONVERT OF LOS ANGELES WOMAN, AND THAT HE HAS THE ONLY REAL GIFT.

MISS IVEY CAMPBELL

> Rocks rained on the roof, and a cat was thrown through the window. Somebody threw a rotten egg at Papa while he was preaching, but with his style of preaching he was a moving target and hard to hit. But it got rougher. Shots were fired over the roof and one night a big railroad tie came scooting down the aisle. But we always had a packed church anyway. For those who dared to attend the services, God more than made up for the persecution.[44]

Perhaps the most painful persecution came from other Christians who said that Pentecostal practices, particularly speaking in tongues, was of the devil. In 1912, the well-known Bible commentator H. A. Ironsides denounced the revival as consisting of "delusions and insanities" that cause a "heavy toll of lunacy and infidelity."[45] The well-known Bible exegete and teacher G. Campbell Morgan referred to the revival as "the last vomit of Satan."[46] In 1941, Louis Bauman declared, "The first miracle that Satan ever wrought was to cause the serpent to speak in a tongue. It would appear he is still working his same original miracle."⁴⁷ As one historian has said, "It could be asserted that no other religious

expel the Pentecostals, and they eventually found full acceptance within the organization. Soon, Pentecostals constituted the majority of NAE membership.

> *"It could be asserted that no other religious movement has suffered more persecution in twentieth-century America, with the possible exception of the Jehovah's Witnesses."*

movement has suffered more persecution in twentieth-century America, with the possible exception of the Jehovah's Witnesses."⁴⁸

## ACCEPTED BY OTHER EVANGELICALS

Instead of destroying the fledgling Pentecostal movement, persecution seemed to fuel its growth. The sheer numerical size of the movement began to demand the attention and respect of non-Pentecostal Christians. In 1942, Pentecostals were cautiously accepted into the newly formed National Association of Evangelicals (NAE). The NAE was formed as an association of theologically conservative churches who wanted to take a middle road between rigid fundamentalism and liberalism. Although Pentecostals comprised only 10 percent of the attending delegates at the founding meeting, their acceptance stirred immediate controversy. Carl McIntire, founder of the American Council of Christian Churches, offered to merge his organization with the NAE if they would "get rid of the tongues groups." The NAE refused to

## ACCEPTANCE BY THE WORLD COUNCIL OF CHURCHES

In 1936, well-known British evangelist Smith Wigglesworth walked into the office of thirty-one-year-old South African David du Plessis and delivered this prophecy:

> I have been sent by the Lord to tell you what He has shown me this morning. Through the old-line denominations will come a revival that will eclipse anything we have known throughout history. You will live to see this work grow to such dimensions that the Pentecostal movement itself will be a light thing in comparison with what God will do through the old churches. You will have a very prominent part. All He requires of you is that you be humble and faithful under all circumstances. If you remain humble and faithful, you will live to see the whole fulfilled.

**THE PRAYER OF FAITH**
*Smith Wigglesworth lays hands on sick child at Angelus Temple in Los Angeles, California, c. 1929.*

## TARRED AND FEATHERED

*Frank Gray, 1947*

Frank Gray was one of the early Pentecostal leaders who bore the brunt of physical persecution. His son, Harold F. Gray, writes,

*It was in early 1918 that a wave of persecution was directed toward my father by some of the neighbors in the farming area where we lived, about 20 miles*

*west of Spokane, Washington. The hatred in these men increased until one evening a group came to the house and forcibly removed him, and took him out and literally "tarred and feathered" him. I was sleeping at the time he came home, but I heard noises downstairs, and I came and saw my mother scraping the tar from his body and bathing him.*⁴⁹

## REVIVAL MAY BRING DISRUPTIVE CHANGE

David du Plessis gave the plenary address at the 1948 Pentecostal World Conference held in Zurich, Switzerland. He urged his audience to pray for revival and then exhorted them to be ready for a spiritual upheaval when their prayers were answered. He said, "Nothing can take the place of the Holy Spirit in the church. So let us pray for a greater outpouring of the Holy Spirit than ever before. And remember, when the flood comes, it will not keep to our well-prepared channels, but will overflow and most likely cause chaos in all our programs."

In 1948 du Plessis moved his family to the United States, and in 1952 he became the interim pastor of Stamford Gospel Tabernacle in Stamford, Connecticut. That same year he sensed the Holy Spirit directing him to visit the World Council of Churches (WCC) headquarters in New York City. Du Plessis warily obeyed and was pleasantly surprised when the officials at the WCC received him with open arms and urged him to tell them about Pentecostalism.

Through his contact with the WCC, du Plessis became friends with John MacKay, president of Princeton Theological Seminary and a respected leader

**MR. PENTECOST**
*David du Plessis became an ambassador of Pentecost to liberal and mainline churches*

in the WCC. MacKay introduced du Plessis to others in the WCC and arranged for him to attend WCC gatherings and address certain venues. Du Plessis obtained great favor with the WCC and in the following years presented lectures on Pentecostalism at Princeton Theological Seminary, Yale Divinity School, Union Theological Seminary, and other liberal institutions that had been considered off-limits to Pentecostals. His ministry to the liberal churches earned him the title Mr. Pentecost and helped prepare the way for the Charismatic renewal of the 1960s and 1970s.

## THE THIRD FORCE

The growing recognition and acceptance of the Pentecostal movement was further highlighted by an article published in the June 1958 edition of *Life* magazine entitled "The Third Force in Christendom." Author Henry Van Dusen, president of the liberal Union Theological Seminary, argued that the incredible growth of Pentecostalism had resulted in it becoming a "third force" in Christendom alongside Roman Catholicism and

would probably feel more at home at a Pentecostal revival than in the formalized worship of other churches, Catholic or Protestant.[50]

Social acceptance and affluence, however, seemed to come with a price. As the movement gained acceptance, it seemed to lose spiritual vitality and power. The 1930s and 1940s have been described as a time when "the depth of worship and the operation of the gifts of the Spirit so much in evidence in earlier

*"...Peter, Paul, and Barnabas would probably feel more at home at a Pentecostal revival than in the formalized worship of other churches, Catholic or Protestant."*

**UNEXPECTED DEFENDER**
*Henry Van Dusen (pictured in 1950), president of Union Theological Seminary, called Pentecostals a "third force" in Christendom and defended them against their Christian critics.*

Protestantism. He also sharply criticized the traditional churches for referring to the various Pentecostal groups as "fringe sects." "On the fringe of what?" he asked. "Perhaps on the fringe of traditional churches, but not necessarily on the fringe of Christendom." Van Dusen went on to suggest that Peter, Paul, and Barnabas

decades were not so prominent."[51] Many were so concerned that they called for systematic times of prayer and fasting to pray for spiritual renewal and revival. The answer to their prayers seemed to be the Healing revival that began in 1946, the Latter Rain revival that began in 1947, and the Charismatic renewal that began around 1960.

**THE THIRD FORCE**
*The growing revival
leads to acceptance
of Pentecostalism
as a third force.*

**ORAL ROBERTS**
*Early Oral Roberts' tent meeting.*

# The Healing Revival

# THE HEALING REVIVAL

**VOICES OF HEALING**
*(l-r) Young Brown, Jack Moore, William Branham, Oral Roberts, and Gordon Lindsay in the 1950s.*

**W**ILLIAM BRANHAM (1909–1965) WAS A BAPTIST MINISTER IN JEFFERSONVILLE, INDIANA, WHO MOONLIGHTED AS A GAME WARDEN BECAUSE THE SMALL CHURCH HE WAS PASTORING WAS UNABLE TO SUPPORT HIM AND HIS FAMILY. ACCORDING TO BRANHAM, AN ANGEL APPEARED TO HIM AT 11:00 P.M. ON MAY 7, 1946, AFTER A TIME OF PRAYER AND INSTRUCTED HIM TO CARRY A GIFT OF HEALING TO THE WORLD. THE ANGEL SAID:

> Fear not. I am sent from the presence of Almighty God to tell you that your peculiar life and your misunderstood ways have been to indicate that God has sent you to take a gift of divine healing to the people of the world. If you will be sincere, and can get the people to believe you, nothing shall stand before your prayer, not even cancer.[52]

Branham immediately launched into a limited but successful evangelistic and healing ministry. Jack Moore, a Oneness Pentecostal from Shreveport, Louisiana, saw Branham's potential and gift and introduced him to Gordon Lindsay, an Assemblies of God pastor in Ashland, Oregon. Lindsay, well known and highly respected in Pentecostal circles, agreed to serve as Branham's campaign manager. Lindsay's ability to organize citywide campaigns thrust Branham into international prominence.

# THE OPERATION OF SPIRITUAL GIFTS

Gordon Lindsay related an incident that illustrates the operation of the gifts of healing and the word of knowledge in the ministry of William Branham. He said:

> In one case I recall that a little deaf boy came to be prayed for. Unfortunately, he was so far back in the line that by the time he got near Brother Branham, the service was closed. The lad and his mother looked so sad and disappointed that Jack Moore turned to me and said, "Why don't you pray for him? So I went ahead and prayed for him and God delivered him. The next day he and his mother were back and they got in the prayer line again. As we saw them in the line again, I looked at Brother Jack Moore and he looked at me. Then he said, "I guess it doesn't do us any good to pray for the people. They aren't satisfied unless Brother Branham prays for them." We watched with interest, nonetheless, to see how Brother Branham would handle the case. When the boy came to him, we were startled to hear him say, "Go your way. A man of faith prayed for you last night and you are healed."[53]

**BRANHAM'S CAMPAIGNS**
*William Branham at the pulpit during a healing campaign in Kansas City, Kansas, April 1948.*
Photo courtesy of *Flower Pentecostal Heritage Center*

Branham operated in a particularly powerful ministry of the word of knowledge. When this gift manifested, he often revealed intimate details of the person's life to whom he was ministering. Dr. Walter Hollenweger (1927– ), professor of missions at the University of Birmingham, England, served as Branham's interpreter in Europe on several occasions. In his work *The Pentecostals* he writes:

> The author, who knew Branham personally and interpreted for him in Zurich, is not aware of any case in which he was mistaken in the often detailed statements he made. It was characteristic of Branham's kind-heartedness that he gave certain personal revelations to those who were seeking healing in a whisper, so that they could not be picked up by the microphone and revealed to the spectators.[54]

One of the most dramatic healings that occurred in the Branham campaigns was that of the former congressman from Georgia, William D. Upshaw. Upshaw's condition was well known, as he had served four terms in Congress and had once run for president. At the time of his healing he had been on crutches for sixty-eight years as the result of an accident that occurred when he was eighteen. Upshaw attended Branham's meetings in Los Angeles, where Lindsay encouraged him to trust God for his healing. Two years later Branham told Lindsay of a vision he had seen of a statesman being healed. The following night, as Branham was leaving the platform, he suddenly said, "The congressman is healed." Upshaw rose to his feet and walked unaided for the first time in sixty-eight years. He later testified, "I laid aside my crutches and started toward my happy, shouting wife…and the bottom of heaven fell out. Heaven came down our souls to greet me and glory crowned the mercy seat."[55]

Photo courtesy of *Flower Pentecostal Heritage Center*

**HEALING REVIVAL**
*Ministers and their wives gather at First Assembly of God in Kansas City, Kansas, in December 1950 for the Voice of Healing convention. Among them, Jack Coe (second row, far left), Freda Lindsay (second row, far right), Jack Moore (third row, far left), David du Plessis (third row, second from left) and Gordon Lindsay (fifth row, far left).*

# ORAL ROBERTS

About this time, God was dealing with Oral Roberts, a divinity student at Phillips University and pastor of a small Pentecostal Holiness Church in Enid, Oklahoma. In 1935, when Roberts was seventeen, he had been miraculously healed of advanced tuberculosis. God had spoken to him at that time saying, "I have called you to take My healing power to your generation." Now Roberts was diligently seeking God for a fresh outpouring of the Holy Spirit in his own life and ministry and for the fulfillment of that call.

On May 14, 1947, following a seven-month season of focused prayer and fasting, Roberts received an inner assurance that God's call would begin to be fulfilled.[56] At this time, God also revealed to Roberts that he would feel His power in his right hand and that as he laid his hands on the sick, he would be able to detect the name and number of any demons present.

Roberts launched into ministry, emphasizing physical healing and salvation for the soul. His ministry was an instant success. In 1948, to accommodate the crowds, he ordered a tent to seat 2,000. The crowds increased, and by 1953, he was conducting meetings under a tent that seated 12,500. Remarkable miracles occurred, and Roberts became the most prominent healing evangelist of that era.

All photos courtesy of Oral Roberts University Photography Dept.

**TELEVISED TENT MEETINGS**
*Oral Roberts' healing ministry, which began in 1947, helped bring the Healing revival to national attention. Thousands crowded into his tent to participate in meetings and to be healed. Many of his services were televised, and in a very short time Roberts became the face of the Healing revival to millions.*

## *In His Own Words*
## ORAL ROBERTS' TESTIMONY OF HEALING FROM TUBERCULOSIS

*My eldest brother visited me. "Get up, Oral," Elmer said. "I am taking you to a revival meeting where a man is praying for the sick." "I can't get up," I said. "I haven't been able to walk in months." "I'll carry you," he said, and dressed me and put me on a mattress in the back seat of the car he was driving. When the evangelist prayed for me that night, he prayed in the name of the "mighty Jesus of Nazareth" and commanded, "You foul sickness, come out of this boy." At first there was a warmth like warm water coming over me. It went into my lungs. I took a deep breath, and I could breathe all the way down. I knew that a miracle was starting. In a few moments time I was standing straight and tall. I was breathing down deep. I was talking. I was a healed man and in my heart God's voice was ringing: "Son, I am healing you, and you are to take My healing power to your generation."[57]*

# VOICE OF HEALING

The ministries of William Branham and Oral Roberts signaled the beginning of a significant era of healing evangelism. Almost immediately, a host of other evangelists began reporting miraculous healings and other supernatural phenomena in their meetings. These included A. A. Allen, Jack Coe, T. L. Osborn, William Freeman, W. V. Grant, Kenneth Hagin, and many others.

Lindsay, who separated from Branham in 1955, gave cohesion and publicity to the revival through his *Voice of Healing* magazine and annual Voice of Healing conventions. One writer described his role in the revival as "the conductor of an unruly orchestra."[58]

**RESPONDING IN FAITH**
*A large group gathers at a music hall in Kansas City, Missouri, for the Voice of Healing convention, December 1950.*
Photo courtesy of Christ For The Nations

Jack Coe, c. 1951.

A. A. Allen, c. 1960.

Photos courtesy of *Flower Pentecostal Heritage Center*

# FREDA LINDSAY AND CHRIST FOR THE NATIONS

GORDON LINDSAY (1906–1973), who guided the Healing revival during the 1950s and 1960s, founded a Bible school in Dallas in 1970 that he called Christ For The Nations Institute. In April 1973 Gordon died suddenly on the platform of the school auditorium while his wife, FREDA (1914– ), was making announcements. The board of directors voted Freda in as president, and under her leadership the school and ministry flourished. Christ For The Nations now sits on an eighty-acre campus in the Oak Cliff section of Dallas. The school offers a two-year institute program and third-year specialty schools of missions, leadership, worship, youth, and children. The ministry is known for its praise and worship recordings and its missions emphasis. Almost thirty thousand students have studied at CFNI. Freda turned the reins of the school and ministry to her son, Dennis, and lives in a campus apartment and serves as president emeritus.

# T. L. AND DAISY OSBORN

In 1945, T. L. AND DAISY OSBORN (1923– ; 1924–1995) went to India as Pentecostal missionaries but were unable to persuade people to believe in the Lord Jesus Christ. The young couple returned to America determined to find a more effective way of spreading the gospel. While pastoring in the Northwest they attended a William Branham campaign in their city and saw the power of God at work. After much prayer and fasting, they launched into their own healing ministry emphasizing Hebrews 13:8, which says that Jesus Christ is the same yesterday, today, and forever.

As they began holding evangelistic and healing crusades, signs and wonders followed, and the Osborns believed they had found the right means of spreading the gospel. Following a period of cooperative ministry with the Voice of Healing in America, the Osborns returned to the mission fields of the world. Traveling to seventy-six nations, they pioneered mass healing crusades with phenomenal results. They found that demonstrations of God's compassion and healing power caused thousands to accept Christ in a single service. Their pioneering approach to miracle evangelism became a model others followed in later decades, and it caused the Pentecostal-Charismatic movement to grow rapidly in third world nations where two out of every three Christians would soon identify themselves as a Pentecostal-Charismatic.

**MIRACLE MINISTRY**
*(clockwise from left) T. L. Osborn with a man healed of paralysis in both legs at a 1985 Uganda crusade.*
*Daisy Osborn with a formerly blind Muslim man who was healed in a Mombasa, Kenya, crusade in 1986.*
*The Osborns lead a group bearing projectors and film equipment to help them evangelize remote tribes in Papua, New Guinea, in 1971.*
*The Osborns with a woman healed of blindness at a 1949 tent meeting in Reading, Pennsylvania.*
*A man holds leg braces and a special shoe he had worn before being healed in a Trinidad crusade in 1965.*

## ORAL ROBERTS UNIVERSITY

While having dinner in a public restaurant, Oral Roberts heard the voice of God speaking to him, "Build Me a university. Build it on My authority and the Holy Spirit. Teach your students to hear My voice, to go where My light is dim. Their work will exceed yours, and in this I am well pleased." Roberts quickly scribbled the words on a napkin, and they became the central message and mission for the university he would build. Roberts began the university in 1965 and received regional accreditation in a record six years. Dedicated by Billy Graham in 1967, ORU now offers a number of degree programs including liberal arts, business, nursing, communications, and theology. Both graduate and undergraduate schools are now in operation. In the middle of the campus sits the prayer tower with the eternal flame burning at the top, highlighting Roberts' desire for prayer to be central at the university. With an average enrollment of 4,600, ORU is considered by many to be the premier Charismatic university in America. In 1993 Richard Roberts was installed as president of the university, and Oral Roberts retained the title of chancellor.

By the end of 1956, the Healing revival was torn by strife between certain healing evangelists and the Pentecostal denominations to which they belonged. Some strife arose from the denominations' jealousy, but some resulted from some evangelists' questionable practices. The revival waned, and a period of crisis followed for many healing revivalists, causing some to quit the ministry. Among those who continued were Gordon and Freda Lindsay; Oral Roberts, who founded Oral Roberts University in Tulsa; the Osborns; and Kenneth Hagin, who founded Rhema Bible Training Center in Broken Arrow, Oklahoma.

As the Healing revival tapered off, the Charismatic renewal began and soon attracted an even larger and more receptive audience. The Healing revival provided an important link between the Pentecostal movement and the Charismatic renewal. Several prominent leaders from the Healing revival became instrumental in the Charismatic movement.

**FATHER AND SON**
*Chancellor Oral and President Richard Roberts, Oral Roberts University*
All photos on this page courtesy of *Oral Roberts University Photography Dept.*

# THE LATTER RAIN REVIVAL

Almost parallel with the postwar Healing revival another revival took place—the Latter Rain revival, which began among students and staff of Sharon Bible College in North Battleford, Saskatchewan, Canada. The school's teachers had visited revival services conducted by William Branham in Vancouver, British Columbia.[59] Deeply impressed by Branham's demonstration of the word of knowledge and by the miraculous healings, the community at Sharon began fasting, praying, and studying the Scriptures with heightened expectation. On February 12, 1948, they experienced an unusual demonstration of God's presence and power. Ern Hawtin, a faculty member at the time, describes what happened.

> Some students were under the power of God on the floor, others were kneeling in adoration and worship before the Lord. The anointing deepened until the awe of God was upon everyone. The Lord spoke to one of the brethren. "Go and lay hands upon a certain student and pray for him." While he was in doubt and contemplation one of the sisters who had been under the power of God went to the brother saying the same words, and naming the identical student he was to pray for. He went in obedience and a revelation was given concerning the student's life and future ministry. After this a long prophecy was given with minute details concerning the great thing God was about to do. The pattern for the revival and many details concerning it were given.[60]

The students spent the next day searching the Scriptures for insight and confirmation of the previous day's events. On February 14:

> It seemed that all heaven broke loose upon our souls, and heaven came down to greet us. Soon a visible manifestation of gifts was received when candidates were prayed over, and many as a result were healed, as gifts of healing were received.[61]

Church historian Richard Riss says the events at Sharon raised hope and interest particularly because of the dearth of manifestations in Pentecostalism between 1935 and 1947. The curious and spiritually hungry flocked to North Battleford from across America and around the world. *The Sharon Star* carried reports and advertised camp meetings and conventions. Before long, Sharon faculty members were responding to invitations to minister throughout North America.[62]

**LATTER RAIN LEADERS**
*Sharon Bible College (top, c. 1950) in North Battleford, Saskatchewan, Canada, became a center of the Latter Rain revival. (bottom, l-r) Herrick Holt with Percy G. Hunt and George Hawtin at groundbreaking service for Sharon Orphanage and Schools, c. 1948.*

Photos courtesy of *Flower Pentecostal Heritage Center*

**NEWS OF REVIVAL**
The Sharon Star *was the voice of the Latter Rain revival.*

## INCREASE AND OPPOSITION

The revival quickly garnered support. In January 1949, Pentecostal pioneer STANLEY FRODSHAM (1882–1969) visited Bethesda Missionary Temple in Detroit at the invitation of its pastor MYRTLE D. BEALL (1896–1979), who had recently embraced the revival. Frodsham, ordained with the Assemblies of God and editor of the denomination's *Pentecostal Evangel*, was impressed by what he saw and became a supporter of the revival. A number of other well-known ministers and organizations also embraced the revival, including Reg Layzell of Glad Tidings Temple in Vancouver, British Columbia; Ivan and Minnie Spencer of Elim Bible Institute, Lima, New York; Zion Evangelistic Fellowship in Providence, Rhode Island; Lewi Pethrus of Sweden; and many others.[63]

The revival emphasized the laying on of hands for the impartation of spiritual gifts, the recognition of apostles and prophets in the present-day church, the gift of prophecy for directing and commissioning ministerial candidates, and "proper" church government. These practices, though they had been common among early Pentecostals, were rejected by many Pentecostal denominations.[64] As a result, some ministers, including Frodsham, left their denominations to work as independent ministers or to join loosely formed fellowships. Although rejected by Pentecostal denominations, these Latter Rain believers influenced and were, to a degree, absorbed into the Charismatic renewal of the 1960s and 1970s.[65]

All photos courtesy of *Flower Pentecostal Heritage Center*

**INVITATION TO REVIVAL**
*Myrtle D. Beall, pictured in the 1950s, was pastor of Bethesda Missionary Temple and an early supporter of the Latter Rain movement.*

**BOLD STEP**
*Stanley Frodsham, pictured in the 1930s, left the Assemblies of God and his editorship of the* Pentecostal Evangel *to join the Latter Rain revival.*

**THE FAITHFUL**
*Camp meeting at Big Bear Lake, California, c. 1936.*

# THE CHARISMATIC RENEWAL

# THE CHARISMATIC RENEWAL

IN APRIL 1960, *TIME* MAGAZINE CARRIED THE STORY OF AN EPISCOPAL PRIEST IN VAN NUYS, CALIFORNIA, WHO HAD BEEN BAPTIZED IN THE HOLY SPIRIT AND HAD SPOKEN IN TONGUES WHILE PRAYING IN HIS HOME. DENNIS BENNETT (1917–1992), RECTOR OF ST. MARK'S EPISCOPAL CHURCH, TOLD HIS CONGREGATION ABOUT THE EXPERIENCE AND SUDDENLY BECAME THE PUBLIC FACE OF A NEW PENTECOSTAL-STYLE MOVEMENT TAKING PLACE IN SO-CALLED "HISTORIC" CHURCHES. OTHER NEWS AGENCIES PICKED UP THE STORY, AND BENNETT'S BAPTISM MARKED THE BEGINNING OF THE MODERN CHARISMATIC RENEWAL.

*In His Own Words*

## ...DENNIS BENNETT'S BAPTISM IN THE HOLY SPIRIT

[A]s I spoke on [in tongues] . . . my heart began to get happier and happier! The Presence of God that I had so clearly seen in earlier days to be the real reason for living suddenly enveloped me again after the many, many years of dryness. Never had I experienced God's presence in such a reality as now. It might have frightened me except that I recognized it as the same Presence of the Lord that I had sensed when I first accepted Jesus.[66]

Photo courtesy of *Flower Pentecostal Heritage Center*

Although Bennett had considerable support from within his parish, a small group vehemently denounced his Pentecostal activity. He resigned from St. Mark's under pressure and was assigned to the pastorate of St. Luke's Episcopal Church in Seattle. But the outpouring of the Holy Spirit continued, and by 1963 *Christianity Today* estimated that two thousand Episcopalians in southern California were experiencing the charismatic phenomenon of speaking in tongues.

In a sense, Bennett had been sent to the backside of the desert. St. Luke's was on the brink of extinction, having already been shut down twice. But under Bennett, St. Luke's returned from the dead and flourished, becoming one of the strongest churches in the Northwest and an important center of charismatic renewal for Episcopalians and many clergy and laypersons from traditional backgrounds. As with most *neo*-Pentecostals (as the early Charismatics were called), Bennett promoted speaking in tongues as the initial Bible evidence of Spirit baptism.

Soon, people within most of the historic Protestant denominations were experiencing the gifts of the Holy Spirit. Charismatic prayer groups sprang up across the country, and people sang praises, prayed spontaneously, spoke and sang in tongues, and enthusiastically ministered to one another in the various gifts of the Holy Spirit.

## THE CATHOLIC CHARISMATIC MOVEMENT

The Charismatic movement spread to the Roman Catholic Church, where the groundwork had been firmly laid by the Vatican II Council (1962–1965). Pope John XXIII, in calling the Council, said he desired the dawning of a new Pentecost that was "the hope of our yearning."[67] He also directed the churches to pray that the Holy Spirit would renew His wonders "in this our day as by a new Pentecost."[68]

*Vatican II Council (1962–1965)*

**CATHOLIC VOICE FOR PENTECOST**

*At Vatican II Council, Cardinal Suenens argued in favor of a charismatic dimension in the life of the church. As a result, the Council declared that the charismatic gifts "should be recognized and esteemed in the Church of today."*

Vatican II's careful acceptance of those outside the Roman Catholic fold invited new opportunities for interaction with non-Catholic Christians. Instead of using the harsh term "heretic," which had been employed for centuries, it chose the phrase "separated brethren" in referring to non-Catholic Christians. It also declared that Christians of other denominations "are joined with us in the Holy Spirit, for to them also he gives his gifts and graces." These statements opened the way for non-Catholic Christians to lead many Roman Catholics into the baptism in the Holy Spirit.[69]

Equally important was the Council's attitude concerning charismatic gifts. When the subject arose for discussion, Cardinal Ruffini expressed the traditional Roman Catholic view that such gifts today "are extremely rare and altogether exceptional."[70] Contrariwise, Cardinal Suenens pointed out that the charismatic dimension, according to St. Paul, is necessary to the church. These gifts are "no peripheral or accidental phenomenon in the life of the Church"; on the contrary, he said, they are "of vital importance for the building up of the mystical body."[71] As a result of Cardinal Suenens' influence, the Council adopted a receptive position on the *charismata*, declaring that these gifts "should be recognized and esteemed in the Church of today."[72] With this foundation in place, as Synan says, "It was almost inevitable that Pentecostalism would break out in the Roman Catholic Church."[73]

The Charismatic renewal in the Roman Catholic Church began at a weekend prayer retreat in 1967 that was attended by about twenty students and a few professors from Duquesne University in Pittsburgh, Pennsylvania. The weekend gathering was held at a large retreat house known as the Ark and the Dove, and the participants had been asked to read the Book of Acts, John and Elizabeth Sherrill's *They Speak With Other Tongues*, and David Wilkerson's *The Cross and the Switchblade*.[74]

**A NEW PENTECOST**

*Pope John XXIII, in calling the Vatican II Council, directed the churches to pray that the Holy Spirit would renew His wonders "in this our day as by a new Pentecost."*

Photo courtesy of *Catholic News Service*

On Saturday evening, after they devoted the day to prayer and study, student David Mangan made his way to the chapel. He later recalled:

> The next thing I knew I was lying prostrate on the floor crying and feeling such "ecstasy" as I may never feel again. I cried harder than I ever cried in my life, but I did not shed one tear. All of a sudden Jesus Christ was so real and so present that I could feel Him all around. I was overcome with such a feeling of love that I cannot begin to describe it.[75]

Later, the entire group gathered in the chapel for what one writer calls "the first totally Catholic Pentecostal prayer meeting."[76] As they prayed, they spoke in tongues, prophesied, and experienced other charismatic manifestations.[77] Synan, who interviewed many of the participants, says:

> As these Catholic seekers prayed through to Pentecost, many things familiar to classical Pentecostals began to take place. Some laughed uncontrollably "in the Spirit," while one young man rolled across the floor in "ecstasy." Shouting praises to the Lord, weeping and speaking in tongues characterized this beginning of the movement in the Catholic Church.[78]

The fire at Duquesne soon spread to Notre Dame University. Many students received the baptism in the Holy Spirit, including Bert Ghezzi, today the editorial director of the Strang Communications book group. From there the movement spread rapidly, and Catholic Charismatic prayer groups sprang up across the country. By 1970, a Catholic Charismatic conference at Notre Dame attracted thirty thousand Catholic Charismatics. Priests, nuns, and laypeople together sang and prayed in tongues, prophesied, and rejoiced in what God was doing.

**NOTRE DAME**
*Notre Dame University became a center for the Catholic Charismatic movement. In 1970, a Catholic Charismatic conference there attracted 30,000 participants.*

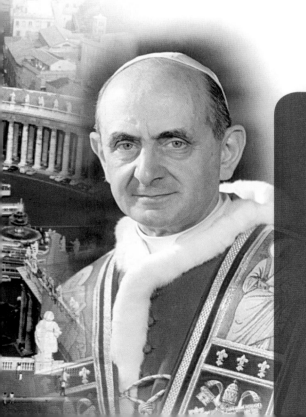

## PENTECOSTAL REVIVAL AT THE HEART OF ROMAN CATHOLICISM

The Charismatic renewal in the Roman Catholic Church reached Rome in 1975 where it received the approval of Pope Paul VI. The pope, addressing a gathering of ten thousand Charismatics at St. Peter's Square, pointed to the positive fruit of the renewal and called it "a chance for the Church and the world." He went on to say, "It will be very fortuitous for our times, for our brothers, that there should be a generation, your generation of young people, who shout to the world the greatness of the God of Pentecost."[79]

**OFFICIAL BLESSING**
*Pope Paul VI told a gathering of 10,000 Charismatics at St. Peter's Square in 1975 that the renewal was "a chance for the Church and the world."*
Photo courtesy of *Catholic News Service*

CANTERBURY CATHEDRAL

## PENTECOSTAL REVIVAL AT THE HEART OF ANGLICANISM

With wide acceptance from the Anglican communion, Anglican Charismatics held an international conference at Canterbury in 1978 to precede the meeting of the Lambeth Conference. Lambeth is the most important gathering of Anglicans, where all bishops meet once every decade. During the week before Lambeth, about five hundred Charismatic leaders gathered at the University of Kent at Canterbury. In the first service, the archbishop of Canterbury and leader of the worldwide Anglican communion, Donald Coggan, addressed the delegates warmly. The closing liturgy was led by Archbishop Burnett and included tongues, prophecies, prayer for the sick, and great rejoicing. This all took place within the context of a traditional Anglican communion service. At the close of this historic gathering, the two thousand worshipers joined in a time of rejoicing as the Spirit was poured out in Pentecostal fullness. Canterbury became for them a new upper room. The ancient walls of the cathedral echoed with shouts of praise. Thirty-two bishops and archbishops danced around the high altar in high praise of the Lord.[80]

# PENTECOSTALS AND CHARISMATICS

Many Pentecostals assumed that these "neo-Pentecostals" would affiliate with their churches. But many neo-Pentecostals found acceptance in their own churches and denominations. In fact, the leaders of this movement saw the revival as God's way of renewing existing denominations. For this reason, they encouraged the people to remain within their churches and, for the same reason, preferred the word *renewal* instead of *revival* to describe their movement.

Although new Pentecostals identified with the older Pentecostals in their experience of the Spirit, there were stark differences in their worship styles and views of church and tradition. Since they were not "Pentecostal" in so many ways, the name "Charismatic" became the common designation for this new movement. The difference between a "Charismatic" and a "Pentecostal" is more historical than doctrinal. Those who identify with churches or groups that began at the turn of the twentieth century are considered "Pentecostal." Those who identify with the renewal movement that began around 1960 or those who choose to remain with the older, traditional churches are generally designated as "Charismatic." By the dawn of the twenty-first century, however, the line between the two had become blurred and the term Pentecostal-Charismatic had become the general designation for all who believe in the miraculous, dynamic working of the Holy Spirit in the church today.

# ECUMENISM AND SCHISMS

Because of the ecumenical character of the Charismatic Renewal, there was extensive fellowship across denominational lines. Conferences were the order of the day, and conference participants normally represented a healthy cross section of Christendom. Catholic priest and scholar Peter Hocken has referred to the movement as "an ecumenical gift of grace poured out on all the churches."[81]

The high-water mark of the renewal occurred in 1977 when fifty-two thousand Pentecostal-Charismatics met in Arrowhead Stadium in Kansas City. Half the registrants were Roman Catholic; the other half Lutherans, Presbyterians, Episcopalians, denominational Pentecostals, Baptists, Methodists, and Messianic Jews. Great rejoicing filled the stands as the multitude sang in tongues and danced before the Lord.[82]

Although Charismatics were encouraged to remain in their churches, many eventually felt they were withering spiritually while others encountered rejection. Many Charismatics left their denominational churches to join classical Pentecostal denominations or to form new, independent Charismatic churches and fellowships. At least three thousand independent Charismatic denominations have been formed worldwide, and their influence and impact are international.

# New Leaders
## and Influences

# NEW LEADERS AND INFLUENCES

A S THE CHARISMATIC RENEWAL BECAME ESTABLISHED, MANY INFLUENTIAL MINISTERS AND PASTORS FROM VARIOUS BACKGROUNDS EMERGED IN THE 1960S AND 1970S TO LEAD THE BROADER PENTECOSTAL-CHARISMATIC MOVEMENT INTO A MORE PROMINENT ROLE IN SOCIETY AND THE CHURCH. RALPH WILKERSON (1927– ) BEGAN PASTORING A CHURCH IN SOUTHERN CALIFORNIA IN 1961 WITH TWENTY-EIGHT PEOPLE. IN 1969, THEY PURCHASED THE THIRTY-SIX-HUNDRED-SEAT MELODYLAND THEATER IN ANAHEIM AND CONVERTED IT INTO MELODYLAND CHRISTIAN CENTER. IT SOON BECAME A CROSSROADS FOR THE RENEWAL AND HOSTED CONFERENCES, HEALING SERVICES, AND SEMINARS ATTENDED BY PEOPLE OF MANY DENOMINATIONAL BACKGROUNDS. MANY TESTIFIED TO HAVING BEEN HEALED AND BAPTIZED IN THE HOLY SPIRIT THERE. IN 1976 WILKERSON FOUNDED MELODYLAND SCHOOL OF THEOLOGY. J. RODMAN WILLIAMS SAYS, "THE CHARISMATIC MOVEMENT REMAINS INDEBTED TO RALPH WILKERSON FOR HIS VISION AND ENERGY IN MAKING POSSIBLE THESE MEMORABLE OCCASIONS."[83]

KATHRYN KUHLMAN (1907–1976) began her ministry at age sixteen and in 1933 established the two-thousand-seat Denver Revival Tabernacle. After a failed marriage, she settled in Pittsburgh, Pennsylvania. In 1946, in Franklin, Pennsylvania, a woman was healed of a tumor in one of Kuhlman's services, marking the beginning of one of the most heralded healing ministries of the twentieth century. Kuhlman did not have prayer lines, but by the word of knowledge would call out healings that were taking place during the service. In 1965 Ralph Wilkerson invited her to minister at Melodyland Christian Center. For ten years she conducted regular healing services with capacity crowds in the seven-thousand-seat Shrine Auditorium. She also used radio and television to further her ministry before her death in 1976.

Photos courtesy of *Flower Pentecostal Heritage Center*

**REVIVAL'S MESSENGERS**
*Melodyland Christian Center (above), became a center for Charismatic conferences in the 1970s. Kathryn Kuhlman (right, and facing page) was one of the most influential healing evangelists of the twentieth century.*

# LEADERS IN THE PENTECOSTAL-CHARISMATIC MOVEMENT

JACK HAYFORD (1934– ) left his post as dean of students at L.I.F.E. Bible College to lead a small Foursquare congregation in Van Nuys, California, in 1969. Through his leadership, the congregation of eighteen members became the ten-thousand-member The Church On The Way, one of America's best-known churches. In 1987 Hayford and The Church On The Way founded The King's College and, later, The King's Seminary. Hayford found wide acceptance among non-Pentecostals and was the plenary speaker at the 1989 Lausanne II Congress on World Evangelism, the only Pentecostal to be afforded this honor. His interdenominational influence has allowed him to build bridges between Pentecostals and evangelicals.[84]

In 1977 ROD PARSLEY (1957– ) began a Bible study with seventeen people in Columbus, Ohio, and prayed, "God, please do things so incredibly large and powerful through this ministry that people will have to look past me to You and say, 'No person could have done this.'" The Bible study became World Harvest Church, which meets in a fifty-two-hundred-seat auditorium.

In 1992, Lester Sumrall passed his "sword of anointing" to Rod and his wife, Joni, conferring on Rod the spiritual mantle of his ministry. Sumrall had received the mantle from Smith Wigglesworth by the laying on of hands.

Today, Parsley is well known through his television program, *Breakthrough*. Parsley also founded the Center for Moral Clarity, an advocacy group that some believe helped George W. Bush win reelection in 2004 by turning out Christian voters in Ohio. Parsley's 2005 book, *Silent No More*, issued a rousing call to Christians to become socially and politically active.

In December 1979 TOMMY BARNETT (1937– ) accepted the pastorate of the First Assembly of God in Phoenix, Arizona, and grew the church from an average attendance of two hundred fifty to a weekly attendance of fifteen thousand, making it one of the largest churches in America. First Assembly stages elaborate dramatic presentations at Christmas, Thanksgiving, Independence Day, and Easter. Special services conducted between Palm Sunday and Easter Sunday recently attracted one hundred fifty thousand people.

In 1994 Barnett launched the Los Angeles International Church, better known as the Dream Center, in partnership with his son Matthew. The church began with forty-eight people and now reaches thirty-five thousand people per week. President George W. Bush visited the Dream Center and declared it to be a prime example of the effectiveness of faith-based social action.

The early life of JOYCE MEYER (1943– ) gave no indication that she would become one of the most popular Bible teachers in the world. Joyce grew up in Appalachia under an abusive father. At age eighteen she left home and entered into a disastrous marriage that ended after twenty separations in five years. At one point she was abandoned and living in a rooming house. In 1967 she married Dave Meyer, a Spirit-filled Lutheran. Joyce struggled in her walk with God but found victory and consistency as she cried out to Him in faith and sincerity. In 1976 she began teaching Bible studies and started her *Enjoyng Everyday Life* radio broadcast, which is now heard on more than two hundred fifty stations nationwide. In 1993 she began her thirty-minute *Enjoyng Everyday Life* television broadcast, now seen across the world. Joyce's relaxed, personal teaching style resonates with people. Millions of her books are in print. Joyce and Dave Meyer make their home in Fenton, Missouri.

BILLY JOE DAUGHERTY (1953– ) and wife, Sharon, founded Victory Christian Center, now one of the most dynamic churches in North America. Daugherty is known for his emphasis on victorious living through faith in God's Word, divine healing, and world missions. Out of Victory Christian Center has emerged Victory Bible Institute, a large Christian academy, a world missions training center, and Victory Fellowship of Ministries. Daugherty also serves as a board member of the Pentecostal Fellowship of North America and chairman of the International Charismatic Bible Ministries.

Reared in a Jewish orphanage in New Jersey, MORRIS CERULLO (1931– ) was supernaturally led to a Christian woman who introduced him to Jesus and the baptism in the Holy Spirit. In the early years of his ministry, Cerullo was associated with the Voice of Healing and became known for his large miracle crusades in third world nations. Cerullo bases his ministry out of San Diego, California, from where he continues to conduct miracle crusades in North America and in other nations.

**HEALING TODAY**
*A Benny Hinn meeting in the Philippines.*

# THE EVANGELISTS

The 1970s and 1980s also saw the rise of Pentecostal-
Charismatic evangelists who drew hundreds of thousands,
even millions of people to crusades around the world.

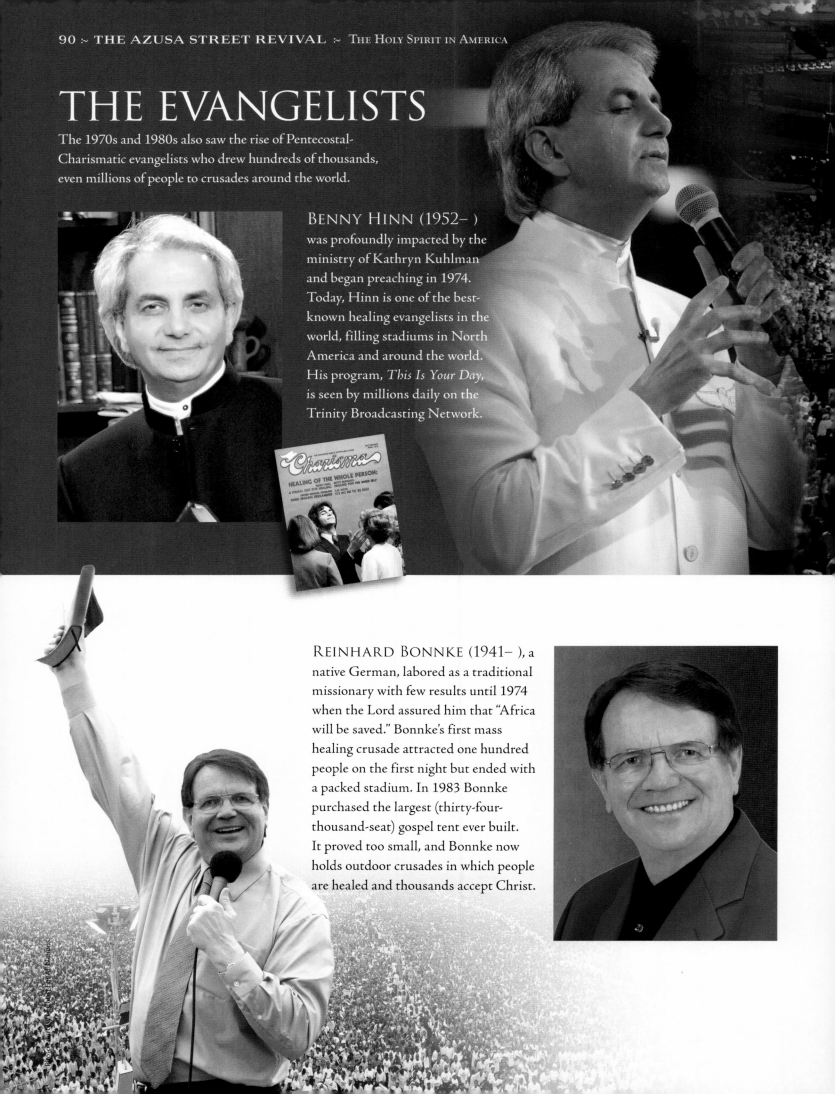

BENNY HINN (1952– )
was profoundly impacted by the
ministry of Kathryn Kuhlman
and began preaching in 1974.
Today, Hinn is one of the best-
known healing evangelists in the
world, filling stadiums in North
America and around the world.
His program, *This Is Your Day*,
is seen by millions daily on the
Trinity Broadcasting Network.

REINHARD BONNKE (1941– ), a
native German, labored as a traditional
missionary with few results until 1974
when the Lord assured him that "Africa
will be saved." Bonnke's first mass
healing crusade attracted one hundred
people on the first night but ended with
a packed stadium. In 1983 Bonnke
purchased the largest (thirty-four-
thousand-seat) gospel tent ever built.
It proved too small, and Bonnke now
holds outdoor crusades in which people
are healed and thousands accept Christ.

**CRUSADE**
*Benny Hinn Crusade at Madison Square Gardens*

Photo courtesy of Benny Hinn Ministries

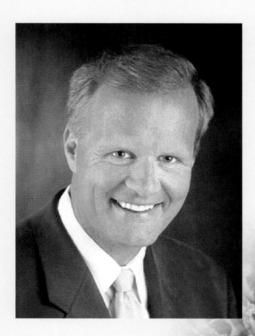

PETER YOUNGREN (1954– ), a native Swede, established one of the most successful churches and ministries in Canada. Youngren conducts several outdoor mass miracle crusades, which he calls "Festivals of Praise," each year in Africa and Asia.

Photo courtesy of World Impact Ministries

**IBADAN, NIGERIA**
*Bonnke's crusades
often draw hundreds of
thousands of people.*

# THE WORD OF FAITH MOVEMENT

As the Charismatic renewal spread and left a lasting imprint on the church, another movement arose emphasizing the importance of God's Word as a counterbalance to the experience of the Holy Spirit. The Word of Faith Movement's pioneer was KENNETH HAGIN (1917–2004), a longtime Pentecostal who was healed of an incurable heart disease at age sixteen by claiming God's promises of healing. Hagin taught that the Bible's promises could be appropriated by confessing and acting upon the promise.

Hagin's message of faith in God's Word found a ready audience among Charismatics. While not denying the validity of subjective, spiritual experiences, Hagin and other faith teachers emphasized that the objective truth of God's Word should have priority over any experience. When Hagin and son Ken Jr. founded Rhema Bible Training Center in 1974, the faith message proliferated through its graduates.

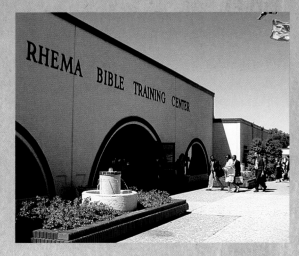

**WORD OF FAITH PIONEER**
*Kenneth Hagin's preaching ministry, Rhema Bible Training Center, and radio broadcasts encouraged millions to live with greater faith.*

- THOUSANDS HAVE RECEIVED ACTIVE POSSESSING FAITH!
- A TEACHING MINISTRY WHICH WILL REVO-LUTIONIZE YOUR LIFE!
- MIRACLES HAPPEN WHICH CHALLENGE, AMAZE AND THRILL THE SOUL!

## A Ministry of Revelation!

**HEAR! Kenneth Hagin**
BEGINNING DATE — APRIL 18, 1956

The amazing visions and revelations from God on:

**First Foursquare Church**
11TH & JUNIPERO AVE.

- HEAVEN
- HELL
- LAST DAYS!

**2 Services Daily**
Bring The Sick for Healing
10 A.M. - "Faith Clinic"
All Welcome
Nursery Provided for all services.

7:30 P.M.
"Messages of
Bible Deliverance"
Prayer for the Sick

FOURSQUARE CHURCH

Dr. and Mrs. Clifford L. Musgrove, Ministers

**BLAZING A TRAIL**
*Many of today's leading ministers were revolutionized by Hagin's teaching on the unalterable truth of God's Word.*

KENNETH COPELAND (1937– ), now the most prominent voice in the Word of Faith Movement, enrolled at Oral Roberts University in 1967 and was a pilot for Roberts in his crusade travel. While in Tulsa, Copeland was heavily influenced by Kenneth Hagin seminars, and in 1968 Copeland and wife, Gloria, returned to Ft. Worth and founded Kenneth Copeland Ministries. In 1973 they began publishing the *Believer's Voice of Victory*, and three years later began a radio broadcast that quickly spread throughout North America. In 1979 the Copelands launched a television broadcast and in 1981 began using satellite communications to take their message around the globe. The Copelands have written numerous books on faith, healing, and prosperity.

**VOICES OF VICTORY**
*Gloria and Kenneth Copeland spread the message of faith through their television broadcasts, conferences, books, and tape ministries.*

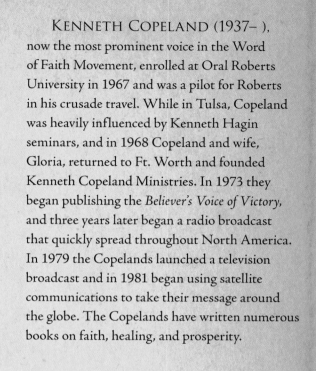

FRED PRICE (1932– ) was reared in a Jehovah's Witness environment but was converted to Christ at a tent crusade in 1953. He entered full-time ministry, embraced Hagin's message, and founded Crenshaw Christian Center in the South Los Angeles area. Later the church purchased a thirty-two-acre campus and completed a new worship center called the FaithDome. Price's multiracial congregation is one of the largest in America with more than twenty thousand members. His national television broadcast, *Ever Increasing Faith*, is seen on more than one hundred twenty-five stations.

**EVER-INCREASING FAITH**
*Betty and Fred Price minister at the 10,000-seat FaithDome in South Los Angeles.*

# PENTECOSTALS DOMINATE THE RELIGIOUS AIRWAVES

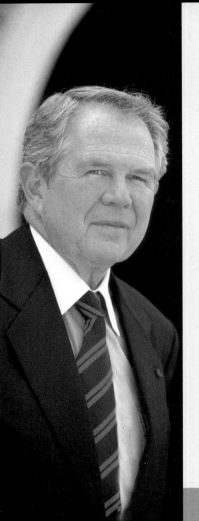

FROM THE TIME AIMEE SEMPLE MCPHERSON PREACHED THE FIRST RADIO SERMON IN 1922 AND ORAL ROBERTS TELEVISED HIS HEALING CRUSADES IN 1954, PENTECOSTALS USED TECHNOLOGY AND MEDIA TO COMMUNICATE THEIR MESSAGE.

## CHRISTIAN BROADCASTING NETWORK

One of the most influential religious media outlets to come out of the Pentecostal-Charismatic movement was the Christian Broadcasting Network (CBN) founded by PAT ROBERTSON (1930– ) in Portsmouth, Virginia, in 1959. CBN grew dramatically and eventually became a major force in cable television with an estimated thirty million subscribers. In 1989 CBN dropped its nonprofit status and became The Family Channel, a commercial stock-owned corporation. In 1997 The Family Channel was sold to media mogul Rupert Murdoch for a reported $1.5 billion. CBN's flagship program, *The 700 Club*, continues to be seen on The Family Channel and other channels. In 1977 Robertson founded CBN University, now known as Regent University, a widely respected Christian university.

## DAYSTAR TELEVISION NETWORK

Daystar Television Network, led by Marcus and Joni Lamb of Dallas, was founded in 1993 with the purchase of channel 29 in Dallas. Daystar now operates forty-five stations in major markets throughout the United States and broadcasts by satellite to two hundred nations.

# TRINITY BROADCASTING NETWORK

The largest Christian television network with around 3,334 stations worldwide is the Trinity Broadcasting Network, founded in 1973 by Paul and Jan Crouch. Paul, the son of Assemblies of God missionaries to Egypt, got his start in broadcasting by splicing together tubes and wires to create a campus radio station while a student at Central Bible College in Springfield, Missouri, in the 1950s. There he met Jan Bethany, whose father was the pastor of a prominent Assembly of God church in Columbus, Georgia. Paul and Jan were married in 1957, and Paul began serving on staff at First Assembly of God in Rapid City, Iowa. To supplement his meager salary, he worked as a disc jockey for a country music station. The station owner opened an NBC television affiliate in Rapid City, and Paul conducted the station's first newscast. In 1961 the Crouches moved to California where Paul helped to produce filmstrips and motion pictures for the Assemblies of God and other denominations. He was briefly involved with a local, church-owned UHF Christian station.

In 1973 the Crouches were able, through a series of miracles, to purchase Channel 40 in Los Angeles, and the Trinity Broadcasting Network was born. Thirty-three years later, TBN is on more than six thousand cable systems and reaches ninety-one million American households, representing 90 percent of the U.S. population.

**A LIFE IN BROADCASTING**
*Paul Crouch started a radio station at Central Bible College (top, l-r), then founded TBN, which received its first FCC license in 1974. Today, TBN reaches the world by satellite.*

**NEW FRONTIERS**
*TBN now beams the gospel to Russia, the Middle East, Africa, Europe, Southeast Asia, India, Indonesia, Brazil, and more.*

**WORLDWIDE REACH**
*Through TBN World Radio and Trinity Music City, USA, the Crouches have diversified and expanded TBN's ministries. Trinity Music City USA in Nashville offers TBN-produced concerts, dramas, seminars, and special events.*

# CROSSROADS CHRISTIAN COMMUNICATIONS

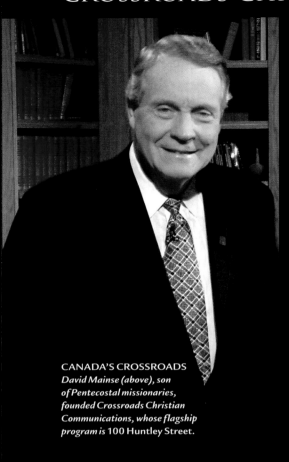

In Canada, Crossroads Christian Communications, Inc., founded by DAVID MAINSE (1936– ), produces programming that is seen across Canada and in at least fifty other nations. Mainse, whose parents were Pentecostal missionaries to Egypt, began his television ministry in 1962 while pastoring a Pentecostal church in Pembroke, Ontario. The flagship program of Crossroads, *100 Huntley Street*, is seen daily across Canada by more than one million viewers.

**CANADA'S CROSSROADS**
*David Mainse (above), son of Pentecostal missionaries, founded Crossroads Christian Communications, whose flagship program is 100 Huntley Street.*

**LEGACY AND FUTURE**
*Ron and Ann Mainse (above) host 100 Huntley Street. At left (top and bottom), David and Norma-Jean Mainse.*

# ROBERT WALKER—PUBLISHING PIONEER

Robert Walker pioneered Christian magazine and book publishing beginning in 1941, when he transformed a floundering publication into *Christian Life* magazine, which became the foremost independent evangelical publication in the United States at the time. It took over other magazines, including *The Way, Religious Digest, Sunday School Digest, Christian Parent,* and *Christian Life & Times,* from which it derived its new name. In 1955, Walker founded *Christian Bookseller* magazine to cover the Christian trade publication industry.

Walker, from the "evangelical mecca" of Wheaton, Illinois, received the baptism in the Holy Spirit in the early 1950s and was one of the first journalists to write about the Charismatic movement. In those years his influence was immense in both religious communities as evangeli-

cals considered him a Charismatic, while the new Charismatics still considered him an evangelical. In 1968, *Christian Life* profiled Hollywood star Pat Boone and described his experience with the Holy Spirit. Later he published a book by Boone, *A New Song,* which sold an astounding 2.5 million copies in six months to readers hungry to learn more about the work of the Holy Spirit.

In 1987, Walker, then seventy-four, merged *Christian Life, Christian Bookseller,* and Creation House Books with Stephen Strang and *Charisma* magazine. Today, Walker's legacy continues through the many publications and books of Strang Communications. Now well into his nineties, Walker is editor emeritus for *Charisma & Christian Life.* Walker once described the role of the Christian journalist with these words: "We've been born of the Spirit... to communicate the good news of Jesus Christ, of life in the Spirit."

*Walker with Billy Graham (above); Mr. and Mrs. Robert Walker.*

# THE THIRD WAVE

In 1983 C. PETER WAGNER (1930– ), then professor of church growth at Fuller Theological Seminary School of World Missions, referred to a "third wave" of the Holy Spirit's work that was already stirring in conservative evangelical churches.

The "first wave," Wagner said, had been the Pentecostal revival at the turn of the century; the "second wave" was the Charismatic renewal, which had influenced liberal denominations and Roman Catholicism. This "third wave," Wagner stated, would have a similar impact on the more conservative evangelicals.[85]

# JOHN WIMBER AND THE VINEYARD

Along with Wagner, JOHN WIMBER (1934–1997) emerged as a recognized spokesman for the Third Wave. Wimber founded the Association of Vineyard Churches beginning with the Vineyard Christian Fellowship of Anaheim around 1977. Wimber traveled widely to minister in teaching and healing, and his meetings were characterized by manifestations of the Holy Spirit similar to what earlier Pentecostals had experienced: people prophesied, spoke in tongues, were "slain in the Spirit," shook, and swooned in a state similar to drunkenness. While emphasizing signs, wonders, and spiritual gifts, Third Wavers often prefer to remain identified with their own denominations. When asked if he considered himself a Pentecostal or Charismatic, Wagner replied:

> I see myself as neither a charismatic nor a Pentecostal. I belong to Lake Avenue Congregational Church. I'm a Congregationalist. However, our church is more and more open to the same way that the Holy Spirit does work among charismatics....We like to think that we are doing it in a Congregational way; we're not doing it in a charismatic way. But we're getting the same results.[86]

Third Wavers also reject, at least theologically, a subsequent experience of Spirit baptism evidenced by speaking in tongues. They prefer, instead, to see Spirit baptism as part of the conversion-initiation experience. In this approach, every convert has the potential to release any of the spiritual gifts. The genuineness of the experience, however, does not hinge on the manifestation of any particular gift.

Although advocating loyalty to denominations, the Third Wave continues to

spawn independent churches and denominations, including the Association of Vineyard Churches, comprising well over three hundred churches throughout North America, and the recently formed Partners in Harvest network of churches, which has formed out of the revival centered in Toronto at the Toronto Airport Christian Fellowship, formerly a part of Wimber's Association of Vineyard Churches.

In spite of the obvious differences among Pentecostals, Charismatics, and Third Wavers, David Barrett, author of the *World Christian Encyclopedia*, sees the Third Wave as part of one great spiritual movement that is sweeping the earth. He says the Pentecostal movement, which began at the turn of the century, the Charismatic renewal, which began around 1960, and the Third Wave are "one single, cohesive movement into which a vast proliferation of all kinds of individuals and communities have been drawn....Whether termed Pentecostals, Charismatics or Third Wavers, they share a basic single experience. Their contribution to Christianity is a new awareness of spiritual gifts as a ministry to the life of the Church."[87]

**DOING THE STUFF**
*John Wimber and his Vineyard churches introduced many people to the gifts of the Spirit.*
Photo courtesy of *Flower Pentecostal Heritage Center*

**REVIVAL IN TORONTO**
*Millions traveled to Toronto Airport Christian Fellowship, pastored by John Arnott, to experience the outpouring of the Holy Spirit.*

BROWNSVILLE
*The glory hits the crowd.*

# RECENT DEVELOPMENTS

# RECENT DEVELOPMENTS

**D**URING THE 1990S REVIVAL MOVEMENTS SPRUNG UP THAT RESEMBLED THE AZUSA STREET REVIVAL WITH THEIR IN-TENSE WORSHIP, RADICAL OPENNESS TO THE HOLY SPIRIT, AND UNUSUAL SPIRITUAL MANIFESTATIONS SUCH AS FALLING, SHAKING, LAUGHTER, AND WEEPING. PEOPLE CAME BY THE MILLIONS TO THESE NEW CENTERS OF REVIVAL.

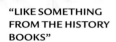

**"LIKE SOMETHING FROM THE HISTORY BOOKS"**
*South African evangelist Rodney Howard-Browne, shown at 1993 meetings at the Carpenter's Home Church in Lakeland, Florida, has been an influential revivalist in the United States. His meetings attract thousands.*

In March 1993, South African evangelist Rodney Howard-Browne arrived at the Carpenter's Home Church in Lakeland, Florida, for a one-week meeting that turned into a fourteen-week revival. Pastor Karl Strader declared it the greatest move of God he had ever seen, "like something from the history books."[88] Spiritual phenomena such as falling, weeping, and joyous laughter occurred nightly and attracted large crowds. By the fourth week of the revival, fifteen hundred converts were baptized. By the end of the sixth week, cumulative attendance had exceeded one hundred thousand, and many pastors and church leaders were profoundly affected.

After fourteen weeks Howard-Browne closed the meetings, saying that God had shown him that the revival in Lakeland was not to become a mecca, but that he was to carry the revival throughout America. After holding similar meetings at Calvary Cathedral International in Fort Worth, Oral Roberts University in Tulsa, and Rhema Bible Institute in Broken Arrow, Howard-Browne returned to the Carpenter's Home Church in Lakeland for a series of meetings in January 1994. Randy Clark, pastor of a Vineyard church in St. Louis, attended, seeking a new level of spiritual power. Clark was profoundly impacted by what he saw and experienced, which included a burning sensation in his hands.

**HUNGER FOR GOD**
*Randy Clark, a pastor from St. Louis, was seeking a fresh enduement of God's power when he visited a service in Lakeland. God used him to spark the revival in Toronto.*

# THE TORONTO BLESSING

Shortly after attending the Howard-Browne meetings in Lakeland, Clark went to Toronto, Ontario, to minister at the Airport Vineyard Christian Fellowship pastored by John and Carol Arnott. There the revival that became known as the Toronto Blessing erupted on Thursday evening, January 20, 1994. Characterized by holy laughter, falling, shaking, divine healings, and other spiritual phenomena, this revival soon captured the attention of Christian and secular media. During the first year of the revival, cumulative attendance exceeded two hundred thousand, and people attended from almost every nation.[89] Secular magazine *Toronto Life* billed the revival as Toronto's top tourist attraction of 1994. By the fall of 1997 attendance had reached two million.[90] In spite of concerns about intense spiritual manifestations, many pastors and church leaders testified that their lives, ministries, and churches were transformed by the renewal. The Toronto Blessing was particularly influential in Great Britain where around seven thousand churches, including many Anglican churches, were profoundly impacted.[91] John and Carol Arnott continue as senior pastors of this church, now known as the Toronto Airport Christian Fellowship.

**REVIVAL OF JOY**
*Revival started on a weekday in January 1994 at a service conducted by Randy Clark (right, ministering in Argentina) at a Vineyard church in Toronto, Canada, pastored by John Arnott (below) and wife, Carol. In subsequent years, millions of people journeyed there to experience an outpouring of the Holy Spirit.*

**MANIFESTATIONS**
*Many people who attended the Toronto revival experienced holy laughter, falling, shaking, divine healings, and other spiritual phenomena.*

# THE PENSACOLA REVIVAL

Another revival with national and international influence began in Pensacola, Florida, at Brownsville Assembly of God on Father's Day, June 18, 1995. Evangelist Steve Hill, who had visited revival centers in Argentina, England,

**REVIVAL LEADERS**
*(l-r) Brownsville Assembly of God pastor John Kilpatrick, worship leader Lindell Cooley, and evangelist Steve Hill.*

and Toronto, preached that morning and invited people up for prayer. During the prayer time many people fell to the floor. Among these was Pastor John Kilpatrick, who lay on the floor for more than three hours. He later testified that he felt all the stress drain out of his body. "I couldn't move, but I felt wonderful," he said.[92]

Spiritual phenomena such as falling, trembling, shaking, laughing, and weeping were common in this revival from that day forward. Kilpatrick had been critical of such phenomena, but said the Holy Spirit told him, "John, if you really want revival, don't tell Me how to do it or when to do it. You'll have to step out of the way."[93]

These manifestations attracted much attention and brought a phenomenal influx of visitors to Pensacola from all over the world. At the revival's height, people waited in line for hours to get a seat at an evening service. The revival was covered by the *New York Times*, the *Washington Post*, PBS, and CNN.

All photos by Cathy Wood

# THE WORLD'S LARGEST CHURCH

**DAVID YONGGI CHO (1936- )** is the founder and pastor of Yoido Full Gospel Church in Seoul, South Korea, the largest congregation in the world with more than seven hundred thousand members. Seven services are held each Sunday in the twenty-five thousand-seat auditorium.

Raised in a Buddhist home, Cho converted to Christianity at eighteen when he was healed of tuberculosis after a young woman prayed for him in the name of Jesus. In 1958 Cho and Ja-Sil Choi, who later became his mother-in-law, founded the Yoido Church in a tent left behind by American Marines. By 1964 the original congregation of five had grown to more than two thousand. Overworked, Cho suffered a nervous breakdown, but during his time of recuperation God gave him a plan for delegating ministry responsibilities. As a result the Yoido Full Gospel Church mushroomed in growth and today has fifty thousand small groups that meet regularly throughout the city. Ninety per cent of the congregational growth comes though these groups, where people are baptized, discipled, and pastored. Cho's church has also blazed trails for women in Korean culture: forty-seven thousand of the small groups are led by women and almost two-thirds of his pastoral staff is female.

In 1976 Cho founded Church Growth International (CGI) as a forum for sharing his biblical principles of church growth. Nearly seven million people have participated in CGI seminars. CGI also has a television ministry, a radio outreach, and a publishing arm. Cho is married to Grace (Kim Sunghae) Cho, an accomplished composer and pianist. They have three grown sons and several grandchildren.

# THE MEMPHIS MIRACLE

Around the time of the revivals in Toronto and Pensacola, a conference later known as the "Memphis Miracle" took place in Memphis, Tennessee. At this meeting the leaders of the all-white Pentecostal Fellowship of North America (PFNA) dissolved their organization, and a new interracial group was formed called the Pentecostal-Charismatic Churches of North America (PCCNA). Bishop Ithiel Clemmons of the Church of God in Christ was elected the new organization's first chairperson.

The highlight of the meeting came when white Pentecostal leaders washed the feet of black Pentecostal leaders and asked forgiveness for the sin of racism among white Pentecostals. Black leaders then washed the feet of their white brothers in a mutual expression of repentance, humility, and forgiveness. This amounted to a public acknowledgment by Pentecostal leaders that the movement had strayed from its interracial roots at the Azusa Street revival.

Participants in the "Memphis Miracle" saw it as the beginning of a new direction in race relations, especially among classical Pentecostals. Many also saw it as a return to the movement's roots. B. E. Underwood, then general superintendent of the International Pentecostal Holiness Church and co-chair of the Memphis event, declared, "We will return with all our hearts to the unity of the Spirit manifested during the blazing revival at Azusa Street." The meeting received much media attention and raised hopes of a new era of racial harmony and spiritual renewal.

**RECONCILIATION**

*Participants in the "Memphis Miracle" saw it as the beginning of a new direction in race relations, especially among classical Pentecostals.*

Photo courtesy of *Flower Pentecostal Heritage Center*

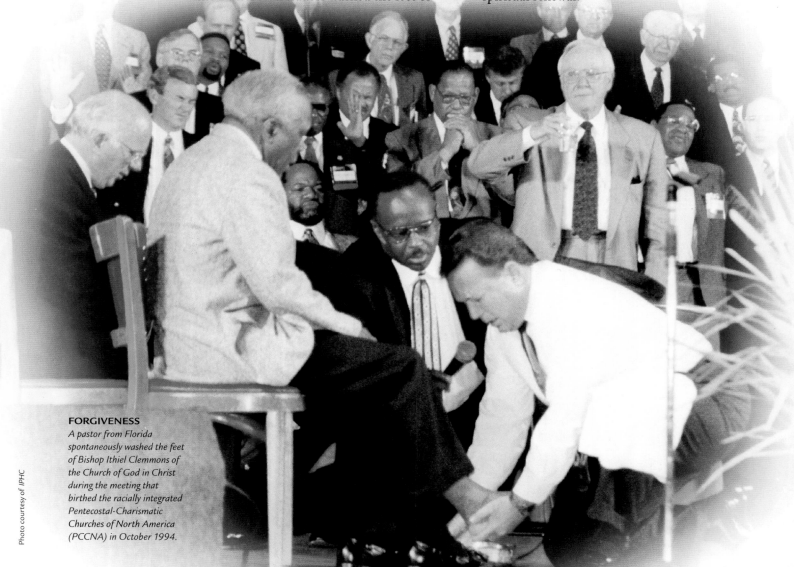

**FORGIVENESS**

*A pastor from Florida spontaneously washed the feet of Bishop Ithiel Clemmons of the Church of God in Christ during the meeting that birthed the racially integrated Pentecostal-Charismatic Churches of North America (PCCNA) in October 1994.*

Photo courtesy of *IPHC*

Photo by Steve Chenn

**LAKEWOOD CHURCH**
*Joel Osteen pastors the largest church in the United States, Lakewood Church in Houston.*

# THE NEXT ONE HUNDRED YEARS

# THE NEXT ONE HUNDRED YEARS

By the beginning of the twenty-first century, the revivals at Toronto and Pensacola had peaked and waned. The crowds became smaller, and revival service schedules were pared back. But the influence of these and other revivals reverberated throughout the church world. Reports of newer Charismatic-type revivals continued to pour in from every corner of the globe. According to Synan, as the twenty-first century dawned, "newer 'Azusa Streets' were popping up in many nations that were spawning mass movements of the Holy Spirit among the masses."[94]

Pentecostal-Charismatics were also moving into positions of influence in society. In 2005, *Time* magazine published a list of what it deemed the twenty-five most influential evangelicals in America. Among them were four well-known Pentecostal-Charismatics: T. D. Jakes, Joyce Meyer, Stephen Strang, and Ted Haggard. Haggard, pastor of New Life Church in Colorado Springs, is also the president of the National Association of Evangelicals and one of the most widely recognized and respected evangelical leaders in America.

Pentecostal-Charismatics have also risen to high levels in U.S. politics. A recent example is John Ashcroft, who served as U.S. senator, governor of Missouri, and attorney general under George W. Bush. Ashcroft is the son of an influential Assemblies of God pastor and educator.

The revival that began in the converted barn at Azusa Street transformed the church forever. Today the Pentecostal-Charismatic movement is growing at a rate of nine million per year. Two-thirds of all Christians in developing nations identify themselves as Pentecostal-Charismatic.[95] Three of the five largest congregations in America are Pentecostal-Charismatic, including Joel Osteen's Lakewood Church in Houston, which has a weekly attendance of twenty-five thousand. Joel is the son of John and Dodie Osteen, who built Lakewood into one of the leading Charismatic churches in the United States, known for its racial integration, worldwide television ministry, and generosity to world missions. Joel continues to build on that foundation. World Changers Church International in College Park, Georgia, is pastored by Creflo Dollar and has a weekly attendance of twenty-three thousand. The Potter's House in Dallas, pastored by T. D. Jakes, has a weekly attendance of eighteen thousand. Four of the five largest churches in the world are Pentecostal-Charismatic, including the mammoth Yoido Full Gospel Church of Seoul, South Korea, which claims more than seven hundred thousand members.

Photo by Steve Chenn

Photo by Billy Bruce

T HE LIVING LEGACY OF AZUSA STREET BELONGS TO THE ENTIRE CHURCH, NOT JUST TO THE PENTECOSTAL-CHARISMATIC MOVEMENT. IN THE NEXT ONE HUNDRED YEARS, SHOULD THE LORD TARRY, THE CHURCH HAS AN OPPORTUNITY TO CONTINUE THE WORK OF THE SPIRITUALLY HUNGRY, HUMBLE PIONEERS WHO WELCOMED THE OUTPOURING OF THE HOLY SPIRIT IN THE TUMBLE-DOWN SHACK IN LOS ANGELES, THEN TOOK THAT POWERFUL AND SPIRIT-FILLED GOSPEL TO THE WORLD.

NOTES

1. Vinson Synan, ed. *The Century of the Holy Spirit* (Nashville: Thomas Nelson, 2001), 371.

2. Tertullian, *Against Marcion*, vol. 3 of *The Ante-Nicene Christian Library*, 447, in Eddie L. Hyatt, *2000 Years of Charismatic Christianity* (Lake Mary, FL: Charisma House, 2002), 16–18.

3. J. Roswell Flower, the first secretary-treasurer of the Assemblies of God, in an article adapted from the *Pentecostal Evangel*, January 29, 1956.

4. *The Apostolic Faith*, vol. 1, no. 2, October 1906.

5. *The Apostolic Faith*, vol. 1, no. 1, September 1906.

6. John G. Lake, *Spiritual Hunger/The God-Men* (Dallas: Christ For The Nations, 1980), 13.

7. "When the Spirit Fell in Los Angeles: An Eye-Witness Account," *Pentecostal Evangel*, April 6, 1946, 6–7.

8. *The Apostolic Faith*, May 1907, compiled by Fred T. Corum, *Like As of Fire* (Wilmington, MA: Corum, 1988), 3.

9. "When the Spirit Fell in Los Angeles: An Eye-Witness Account," 7.

10. Lake, *Spiritual Hunger/The God-Men*, 14.

11. Frank Bartleman, *Azusa Street*, ed. Vinson Synan (Plainfield, NJ: Logos, 1980), 60.

12. *The Apostolic Faith*, vol. 1, no. 1, September 1906.

13. Reprinted from the *Los Angeles Times*, April 18, 1906, 1.

14. Bartleman, *Azusa Street*, 59–60.

15. Ibid., 54.

16. *The Apostolic Faith*, vol. 1, no. 3, November 1906.

17. Stanley M. Burgess, ed. and Eduard M. Van Der Maas, assoc. ed, *The New International Dictionary of Pentecostal and Charismatic Movements* (Grand Rapids, MI: Zondervan Publishing, 2002), 366.

18. Gary B. McGee, "William J. Seymour and the Azusa Street Revival," *Enrichment Journal*, Fall 1999, http://www.ag.org/enrichmentjournal/199904/026_azusa.cfm (accessed October 31, 2005).

19. *The Apostolic Faith*, vol. 1, no. 3, November 1906.

20. *The Apostolic Faith*, vol. 1., no. 4, December 1906.

21. McGee, "William J. Seymour and the Azusa Street Revival."

22. *The Apostolic Faith*, vol. 1., no. 5, January 1907, 3.

23. Stanley Frodsham, *With Signs Following* (Springfield, MO: Gospel Publishing House, 1946), 38–39.

24. Stanley M. Burgess and Gary B. McGee, *Dictionary of Pentecostal and Charismatic Movements* (Grand Rapids, MI: Zondervan, 1988), 110.

25. Vinson Synan, "The Unexpected Transformation of the Pentecostal Holiness Church," *Charisma*, April 1987, 55.

26. Hyatt, *2000 Years of Charismatic Christianity*, 148–154.

27. "The Story of Our Church: The Church of God in Christ—Young C. H. Mason," Church of God in Christ, Inc., http://www.cogic.org/history.htm (accessed October 31, 2005).

28. Frodsham, *With Signs Following*, 107–108, in Hyatt, *2000 Years of Charismatic Christianity*, 156–157.

29. Marie Brown, "I Remember," *Pentecostal Evangel*, March 15, 1964, 20, in Hyatt, *2000 Years of Charismatic Christianity*, 152.

30. Edith Blumhofer, *Pentecost in My Soul* (Springfield, MO: Gospel Publishing House, 1989), 244, in Hyatt, *2000 Years of Charismatic Christianity*, 161.

31. Bartleman, *Azusa Street*, 54.

32. Burgess and McGee, *Dictionary of Pentecostal and Charismatic Movements*, 255.

33. Ibid.

34. Ibid.

35. Ethel E. Goss, *The Winds of God: The Story of the Early Pentecostal Days (1901–1914) in the Life of Howard A. Goss* (New York: Comet, 1958), 168.

36. Gary B. McGee, *People of the Spirit* (Springfield, MO: Gospel Publishing, 2004), 112.

37. Ernest S. Williams, "Memories of Azusa Street Mission," Pentecostal Vertical File, Holy Spirit Research Center Oral Roberts University, 1.

38. Ibid.

39. Burgess and Van Der Maas, *The New International Dictionary of Pentecostal and Charismatic Movements*, 940.

40. Carl Brumback, *Like a River* (Springfield, MO: Gospel Publishing House, 1977), 1.

41. Douglas G. Nelson, "A Search for Pentecostal-Charismatic Roots," (PhD Diss., University of Birmingham, England, 1981), Synopsis.

42. Bartleman, *Azusa Street*, 54.

43. Burgess and Van Der Maas, *The New International Dictionary of Pentecostal and Charismatic Movements*, 984.

44. McGee, *People of the Spirit*, 126.

45. Vinson Synan, *The Holiness-Pentecostal Movement in the United States* (Grand Rapids, MI: Eerdmans, 1971).

46. Vinson Synan, *In the Latter Days* (Ann Arbor, MI: Servant Publications, 1984), 77.

47. Ibid., 76.

48. Ibid., 75.

49. Brumback, *Like a River*, 143.

50. Henry Van Dusen, "The Third Force in Christendom," *Life*, June 6, 1958, 122.

51. Carl Brumback, *Suddenly…From Heaven* (Springfield, MO: Gospel Publishing House, 1962), 331.

52. David Harrell Jr., *All Things Are Possible* (Bloomington: Indiana University Press, 1975), 28.

53. Gordon Lindsay, *God's 20th Century Barnabas* (Dallas: Christ For the Nations, n.d.), 176–177.

54. Walter Hollanweger, *The Pentecostals* (Peabody, MA: Hendrickson, 1988), 354.

55. Lindsay, *God's 20th Century Barnabas*, 179–180.

56. Harrell, *All Things Are Possible*, 42.

57. Oral Roberts, *Twelve Greatest Miracles of My Ministry* (Tulsa, OK: Pinoak Publishers, 1974), 13–14.

58. Harrell, *All Things Are Possible*, 57.

59. Richard Riss, "The New Order of the Latter Rain, A Look at the Revival Movement on Its 40th Anniversary," *Assemblies of God Heritage*, Fall 1987, 15.

60. Ibid., 17.

61. Ibid.

62. Ibid.

63. Ibid.

64. See Corum, *Like as of Fire*, Preface, 6, who states that the official board of twelve at Azusa Street would lay their hands on newly approved ministers and pray "as did the apostles of old. People were told where to go on the mission field through visions and prophecy and results followed wherever they went." See also Richard Riss, "The New Order of the Latter Rain," 16, who lists many of the similarities of the Latter Rain movement with the older Pentecostal movement, including the fact that both were known as the Latter Rain movement.

65. Riss, "The New Order of the Latter Rain," 17.

66. Dennis Bennett, *Nine O'Clock in the Morning* (Plainfield, NJ: Logos, 1970), 24.

67. Edward O'Connor, "Roots of Charismatic Renewal in the Catholic Church," *Aspects of Pentecostal-Charismatic Origins*, ed. Vinson Synan (Plainfield, NJ: Logos, 1975), 183.

68. Ibid.

69. Ibid., 185.

70. Francis A. Sullivan, *Charisms and Charismatic Renewal* (Dublin: Gill and Macmillan, 1982), 4.

71. Ibid., 10.

72. Leon Joseph Suenens, *A New Pentecost?* (N.p.: Darton, Longmen and Todd, 1975), 40.

73. Synan, *In the Latter Days*, 109.

74. Kevin and Dorothy Ranaghan, *Catholic Pentecostals* (New York: Paulist Press, 1969), 24. See also Edward D. O'Connor, *The Pentecostal Movement in the Catholic Church* (Notre Dame: Ave Maria Press, 1971), 38–40.

75. Ranaghan, *Catholic Pentecostals*, 26.

76. Synan, *In the Latter Days*, 110.

77. Ranaghan, *Catholic Pentecostals*, 24–37.

78. Synan, *In the Latter Days*, 111.

79. Vinson Synan, *The Twentieth-Century Pentecostal Explosion* (Lake Mary, FL: Creation House, 1987), 49.

80. Ibid., 95.

81. Peter Hocken, *One Lord One Spirit One Body* (Gaithersburg, MD: The Word Among Us, 1987), 87.

82. Synan, *In the Latter Days*, 128–129.

83. Burgess and Van Der Maas, *The New International Dictionary of Pentecostal and Charismatic Movements*, 1196–1197.

84. Ibid., 692–693.

85. John Wimber, *Power Evangelism* (San Francisco: Harper and Row, 1986), 122–135.

86. Ibid., 134.

87. Burgess and McGee, *Dictionary of Pentecostal and Charismatic Movements*, 818.

88. Julia Duin, "Praise the Lord and Pass the New Wine," *Charisma*, August 1994, 24.

89. Daina Doucet, "What Is God Doing in Toronto?" *Charisma*, February 1995, 21.

90. Fred Wright, interview with author, October 1997.

91. Gerald Coates, letter to author, September 18, 1996; Fred Wright, telephone interview with author, August 26, 1997.

92. Bill Sherman, "Pensacola Revival Reaches Tulsa," *Tulsa World*, May 17, 1997.

93. John Kilpatrick, *Feast of Fire* (Pensacola, FL: John Kilpatrick, 1995), 77.

94. Vinson Synan, "Streams of Renewal at the End of the Century," *The Century of the Holy Spirit*, ed. Vinson Synan (Nashville: Thomas Nelson, 2001), 380.

95. David Barrett, "The Worldwide Holy Spirit Renewal," *The Century of the Holy Spirit*, 381–414; and Burgess and McGee, *Dictionary of Pentecostal and Charismatic Movements*, 810–811.

96. See Gary S. Greig and Kevin Springer, *The Kingdom and the Power* (Ventura, CA: Regal, 1993) for a positive evangelical, Protestant view of the *charismata*.

97. Suenens, *A New Pentecost?*, 40.

# PARTNERS IN
# MINISTRY

# CONTENTS

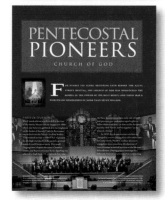

JACK HAYFORD
www.jackhayford.com

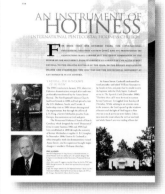

INTERNATIONAL
PENTECOSTAL HOLINESS
CHURCH
www.iphc.org

MARILYN HICKEY
MINISTRIES
www.mhmin.org

JOYCE MEYER
MINISTRIES
www.joycemeyer.org

ROD PARSLEY,
WORLD HARVEST
CHURCH
www.breakthrough.net

FREDERICK K. C. PRICE,
CRENSHAW
CHRISTIAN CENTER
www.faithdome.org

THE CITY CHURCH
www.thecity.org

STRANG
COMMUNICATIONS
COMPANY
www.strang.com

TRINITY
BROADCASTING
NETWORK
www.tbn.org

PETER YOUNGREN,
WORLD IMPACT
MINISTRIES
www.peteryoungren.org

ASSEMBLIES OF GOD · REINHARD BONKKE MINISTRIES ·
CHURCH OF GOD IN CHRIST · KENNETH COPELAND M
CHRISTIAN CENTER · DAYSTAR TELEVISION NETWORK · JO
PENTECOSTAL HOLINESS CHURCH · MARILYN HICKEY MI
HARVEST CHURCH · FREDERICK K. C. PRICE, CRENSH
COMMUNICATIONS COMPANY · TRINITY BROADCASTING N
ASSEMBLIES OF GOD · REINHARD BONKKE MINISTRIES · C
CHURCH OF GOD IN CHRIST · KENNETH COPELAND M
CHRISTIAN CENTER · DAYSTAR TELEVISION NETWORK · JO
PENTECOSTAL HOLINESS CHURCH · MARILYN HICKEY MI
HARVEST CHURCH · FREDERICK K. C. PRICE, CRENSH
COMMUNICATIONS COMPANY · TRINITY BROADCASTING N
ASSEMBLIES OF GOD · REINHARD BONKKE MINISTI
EVANGELISM · CHURCH OF GOD IN CHRIST · KENN
DAUGHERTY, VICTORY CHRISTIAN CENTER · DAYSTA
CK HAYFORD · INTERNATIONAL PENTECOSTAL HOL
MEYER MINISTRIES · ROD PARSLEY, WORLD HARV
CHRISTIAN CENTER · THE CITY CHURCH · STRANG C
NETWORK · PETER YOUNGREN, WORLD IMPACT MI
MINISTRIES · CHURCH OF GOD · MORRIS CERULLO
KENNETH COPELAND MINISTRIES · BILLY JOE AND
DAYSTAR TELEVISION NETWORK · JOHN HAGEE MINIS
HOLINESS CHURCH MARILYN HICKEY MINISTRIES
HARVEST CHURCH · FREDERICK K. C. PRICE, CRENSH

# INTRODUCTION

IN THE CENTURY SINCE THE AZUSA STREET REVIVAL BEGAN, THOUSANDS OF PENTECOSTAL MINISTRIES HAVE BEEN BORN AND HAVE FLOURISHED. NEARLY ALL STARTED AS SMALL, LOCAL CONGREGATIONS OR MINISTRIES SERVING THE NEEDS OF A CERTAIN CITY, TOWN, OR EVEN NEIGHBORHOOD. SOME GREW TO BECOME DENOMINATIONS AND FELLOWSHIPS REPRESENTING MILLIONS OF BELIEVERS. STILL OTHERS BECAME LARGE, INDEPENDENT INTERNATIONAL MINISTRIES TAKING THE SPIRIT-EMPOWERED GOSPEL MESSAGE TO BILLIONS OF PEOPLE BY SATELLITE TELEVISION AND RADIO.

While each Spirit-filled ministry is used by God in wonderfully unique ways, they are all unified by the message of Pentecost that broke forth so powerfully at Azusa Street: that the Spirit of God is loving, powerful, and personally active in people's lives today to save and heal. That message of hope, paired with a godly ambition to take that message to every corner of the globe, has put Pentecostal-Charismatic leaders at the forefront in every area of ministry, from world missions to broadcasting.

The following profiles tell the stories of some of the many ministries that are carrying the banner of revival today. Together, their reach covers billions of people and virtually the entire globe. From evangelists to television ministries to preachers to denominations, the efforts of these ministries on behalf of the gospel represent a broad spectrum of the Pentecostal-Charismatic movement, showing that the vibrancy and promise of the outpouring at Azusa Street live on through the energies of people willing to carry the flame forward today.

# A WORLDWIDE MISSION
## ASSEMBLIES OF GOD

THE ASSEMBLIES OF GOD EMERGED FROM THE EARLY PENTECOSTAL MOVEMENT TO BECOME THE LARGEST PROTESTANT FELLOWSHIP IN THE WORLD WITH FIFTY MILLION ADHERENTS AND MORE THAN TWELVE THOUSAND U.S. CHURCHES. BUT TODAY THERE IS NO SUCH THING AS A TYPICAL ASSEMBLIES OF GOD CONGREGATION. ONE CHURCH MINISTERS TO FORTY PEOPLE IN A RURAL SETTING, WHILE A MEGA-CHURCH REACHES THOUSANDS IN A MAJOR CITY. ONE CONGREGATION WITHOUT A CHURCH BUILDING MINISTERS TO HOMELESS STREET PEOPLE; ANOTHER USES HIGH TECHNOLOGY TO DRAW AN AFFLUENT SUB-URBAN AUDIENCE. BUT ALL ASSEMBLIES OF GOD CHURCHES ARE UNITED IN THEIR COMMITMENT TO EVANGELISM, A PERSONAL RELATIONSHIP WITH JESUS CHRIST, THE BAPTISM IN THE HOLY SPIRIT, PRAYER FOR THE SICK, THE SUPPORT OF MIS-SIONS AROUND THE WORLD, AND STRONG BIBLICAL TEACHING AND PREACHING.

**LEADERSHIP**
*(top) Many early Assemblies of God members trace their Pentecostal heritage to the 1906 Azusa Street revival and William J. Seymour.*
*(middle) Thomas E. Trask has served the Assemblies of God as general superintendent since 1993.*
*(bottom) For twenty-five years Revivaltime radio speaker C. M. Ward's voice was recog-nizable around the world.*

## ORIGINS

The Assemblies of God was born early in the Pentecostal movement, but many Pentecostals rejected the very idea of organizing beyond a local congregation because of their negative experience with established denominational churches. Nevertheless, in 1913, five men—coordinators rather than founders—issued a call to Pentecostals to unite for a common cause. Howard Goss, one of the signers of the call, wrote later, "From the book of Acts, as well as from our own experiences I was led to see that even Spirit-filled people needed some restraint. Just as a good horse still needs a harness to produce worthwhile results, the movement needed a legal form of written cooperative fellowship."

In response, three hundred people assembled in Hot Springs, Arkansas, in April 1914 and enthusiastically formed the General Council of the Assemblies of God. A few months later in Chicago, the delegates to the Second General Council agreed to establish a printing plant, and they ended their two-week conference vowing to see "the greatest evangelism that the world has ever seen."

In 1916 the young organization adopted sixteen essential doctrinal interpretations or explanations, most of which put the Assemblies of God in the center of evangelical Christianity. The statement emphasized the salvation of mankind, the baptism in the Holy Spirit, divine healing, and the blessed hope of resurrection with Christ.

A major doctrinal split only two years into its existence caused the Assemblies of God to lose a third of its ministers. But the fellowship soldiered on and built churches at home and abroad. Congregations met in storefront buildings, former denominational church buildings, tents, brush arbors, in the open air, warehouses, and school buildings. A young Texas pastor and his wife even cleaned out a chicken house for their sanctuary. More often than not, Assemblies of God churches were on the "other side of the tracks," where services were interrupted by the clamor of passing steam engines.

But the fellowship built a strong base. People sought an authentic experience of Christ. They were touched by the worship and

**FIRST MEETING** *(top)*
*A group of leaders from across the country attended the organizational meeting of the Assemblies of God in Hot Springs, Arkansas, in April 1914. A few of the familiar names include John G. Lake, J. Roswell Flower, Ralph Riggs, E. N. Bell, M. M. Pinson, F. F. Bosworth, and Paul Crouch's father, Andrew.*

singing. They saw the sick healed, hardened sinners converted, drunkards delivered, and wayward children and spouses convicted by the Holy Spirit. Families were united around rough altars in humble churches.

## "GREAT EVANGELISM"

From the fellowship's earliest days, social consciousness gripped church members. Lay

**SAVING LIVES**
*David Wilkerson is the founder of Teen Challenge, now ministering around the world to troubled teens and adults.*

people and ordained ministers established skid row missions, clothing and feeding programs, and children's homes from Arkansas to Egypt to India. Teen Challenge, an inner-city program to reach drug addicts, burst on the scene and continues to change thousands of lives. Assemblies of God members founded the Convoy of Hope, which helps victims of disasters around the world.

The Assemblies of God grew into one of the great missionary-sending organizations. Many missionaries spent their entire lives on the mission field. Some gave their lives for the cause of Christ.

Today the Assemblies of God fellowship is far different from that struggling organization of its first decade. It has grown to 2.7 million U.S. adherents. Its churches contribute more than $300 million annually to missions work.

Nineteen colleges and seminaries train ministers and leaders of all kinds. Assemblies of God chaplains minister to people from racetracks to foxholes.

The Assemblies of God family worldwide is helping to carry out "the greatest evangelism that the world has ever seen." What began as a blip on the 1914 church radar screen is now a world-wide force for the advancement of the gospel.

**HOSPITAL IN INDIA** *(top)*
*The Calcutta Mission of Mercy.*
**HEADQUARTERS** *(bottom)*
*The Assemblies of God headquarters complex, Springfield, Missouri, houses the Gospel Publishing House, executive offices, and national departmental offices.*

## Publishing the Pentecostal Message

The Assemblies of God has operated its own printing plant during its entire history, publishing literature that has gone around the world. Its flagship periodical, the *Pentecostal Evangel*, has published weekly for ninety-two years, with a circulation of over two hundred thousand.

# AFRICA'S EVANGELIST

## REINHARD BONNKE

**R**EINHARD BONNKE BECAME KNOWN AS ONE OF THE WORLD'S LEADING EVANGELISTS AS A RESULT OF THE OPEN-AIR GOSPEL CAMPAIGNS HE REGULARLY HOLDS THROUGHOUT THE CONTINENT OF AFRICA, OFTEN DRAWING MORE THAN A MILLION PEOPLE TO A SINGLE EVENT.

The son of a pastor, Reinhard gave his life to the Lord at age nine, and heard the call to the mission field before he was even a teenager. After attending Bible college in Wales, he became a pastor in Germany for seven years and then went on to start a mission work in southern Africa. It was there, in the small mountain kingdom of Lesotho, that God placed upon his heart the vision of "the continent of Africa, washed in the precious Blood of Jesus," an entire continent, from Cape Town to Cairo and from Dakar to Djibouti, that needed to be reached and to hear the proclamation of the signs-following gospel.

**IMPACT**
*On the final evening of a gospel crusade in Jos, Nigeria, more than 650,000 people gather to hear the Word of God. During the week, nearly 1.3 million responded to the call of salvation.*

He began holding meetings in a tent that accommodated just 800 people. As attendance increased, larger and larger tents had to be purchased, until finally, in 1984, he commissioned the construction of the world's largest mobile structure—a tent capable of seating 34,000 people! Soon, attendance at his meetings even exceeded the capacity of this huge structure, and he began open-air gospel campaigns with an initial gathering of more than 150,000 people.

## MILLIONS REACHED FOR THE GOSPEL

Since then, Bonnke has conducted citywide meetings across the continent with as many as 1.6 million people attending a single gathering.

It has now been more than thirty years since Bonnke founded the international ministry Christ for all Nations (CfaN), which currently has offices on five continents. Since the start of the new millennium, through a host of major events in Africa and other parts of the world and with a goal of seeing 100 million souls record a decision for Jesus Christ in this decade, some 40 million have already responded to the gospel call. CfaN has also become an active sponsor in the Global Pastor's Network, a worldwide interdenominational movement that has a vision of reaching one billion souls and planting five million churches around the globe during the next ten years.

**RESULTS**
*Some 1.7 million people made a positive decision for Christ during the five-day Ogbomosho, Nigeria, Gospel Campaign.*

Bonnke is also known for hosting inspirational Fire Conferences, with sometimes as many as 80,000 people in attendance and for distributing more than 90 million copies of "Minus to Plus," a salvation message across entire countries.

As part of the ministry's discipleship training program, more than 178 million copies of CfaN books and booklets have been published in 140 languages and printed in 53 countries. Millions of books have been printed and freely given throughout the world.

Bonnke also operates the Reinhard Bonnke School of Fire, an online self-study course, aimed at inspiring others to Holy Spirit evangelism. He is now developing additional soul-winning projects to inspire the next generation of evangelists through teaching films, encouraging them to reach the unreached, further the kingdom of God, and see the gospel message proclaimed to all nations.

Bonnke's goal remains to use every opportunity, by every possible means, to reach and save the lost. He has a burning passion for the gospel, a vision for the continent of Africa, and a heart for the nations of the world.

**FOCUS**
*Bonnke's goal remains to use every opportunity, by every possible means, to reach and save the lost. Since the start of the new millennium, through a host of major events in Africa and other parts of the world, approximately 40 million people have responded to the gospel call at Bonnke's meetings.*

# APOSTLE TO THE NATIONS

## MORRIS CERULLO WORLD EVANGELISM

**F**OR FIFTY-EIGHT YEARS MORRIS CERULLO HAS PREACHED AN UNCOMPROMISING MESSAGE OF SALVATION, HEALING, AND DELIVERANCE IN NATIONS ACROSS THE WORLD. HE HAS PIONEERED EVANGELISM IN COUNTRIES MANY CONSIDERED CLOSED AND HAS GAINED A REPUTATION AS AN APOSTLE AND PROPHET.

Cerullo was called by God to preach at age fifteen at Bethany Assembly of God in Paterson, New Jersey. According to Cerullo, God took him into the heavens and gave him a supernatural vision, which included a glimpse into hell. From that time on, Cerullo committed his life to helping fulfill the Great Commission and bring in a harvest of souls from around the world.

In 1962, during a crusade in Porto Alegre, Brazil, Cerullo received a mandate from God to build Him an army. God showed Cerullo that the key to evangelizing a closing world was to raise up nationals full of the power of the Holy Spirit who would go into the villages

of their nations. Cerullo made this his driving vision and poured his life into training and equipping nationals through schools of ministry and national conferences. That army of more than 1.5 million nationals around the world is now changing the spiritual destinies of nations.

**PIONEERING IN SOUTH AMERICA**
*(left) In Porto Alegre, Brazil, Cerullo received a mandate from God to build an army full of the power of the Holy Spirit to evangelize the nations. Cerullo has returned many times to South America, including Rosario, Argentina, in 1966 (right).*
*(illustration, above left) An artistic rendition of Cerullo's vision of hell.*

**FULFILLING THE MANDATE**
*(left) Cerullo in Aba, Nigeria, training thousands of believers for ministry in 1974; and in Manila, Philippines, 1989 (right).*

## OPPOSITION

In his early years of ministry throughout Latin America, Cerullo faced tremendous opposition and was arrested and detained many times for preaching the gospel and praying for the sick.

In 1965, when he first went to Argentina, the country was almost completely closed to the gospel, and most attempts to conduct an evangelistic campaign met with persecution. But during Cerullo's crusade in Mar Del Plata, Argentina, so many miracles of healing took place that the College of Doctors accused him of practicing medicine without a license. He continued to minister nightly with

**DECADES OF MINISTRY**
*Cerullo's miracle ministry has spanned decades. (left, top to bottom) Cerullo with crutches in Fortaleza, Brazil, 1968; a woman raised from a wheelchair during a meeting in the 1990s; two deaf girls among the hundreds healed during a crusade in Madras, India, in 1987.*

hundreds of people being saved and healed. The police eventually arrested him and took him to jail. After intensive interrogation, he was released in time to conduct the last night of the crusade.

Those crusades energized Argentina's ministers, many of whom saw for the first time a demonstration of the supernatural power of God. Many who attended went on to build large churches and international ministries.

## BREAKTHROUGHS

In 1970 Cerullo began prophesying that the Iron Curtain would come down. On November 9, 1989, the Berlin Wall was demolished, and Russia and Eastern Europe opened up for evangelism. At this strategic time in 1990, God sent Cerullo to Moscow where ten thousand people packed into the Izmyloski Sports Hall. It was the first evangelistic crusade conducted

in Moscow since the Bolshevik Revolution. Thousands of Russians were saved, and Cerullo spoke on primetime television to a potential audience of twenty million, prayed for the sick, and led viewers in the sinner's prayer.

**MIDDLE EAST OUTREACH**
*Cerullo at an international conference in Amman, Jordan.*

In 1986, during the revolution in the Philippines, God sent Cerullo to Manila with a prophetic word to strengthen the church. There Cerullo trained more than four thousand national believers in a school of ministry.

In 1998 Cerullo conducted seminars and crusades for tens of thousands in Indonesia. God gave him a special prophetic word for the church in Indonesia, saying that, "God is in control, not the government, not Satan. You don't need to worry." Within days Indonesia fell into economic and political disaster. Banks collapsed. Violence erupted, and houses were stripped and burned. But the church was encouraged by the prophetic word God had given them.

In 1999, Cerullo pioneered more spiritual territory. At a meeting of ministers from the Middle East in Amman, Jordan, more than twenty-five hundred people received spiritual breakthroughs that enabled them to reach their countries with the power of God. In 2000, Cerullo met

**MIRACLES**
*(above) A boy paralyzed since birth stood and walked for the first time during a Brazil outreach in 1998.*
*(top right) A deaf boy responded after hearing for the first time during a meeting in London in 1993.*
*(right) Cerullo preached to 10,000 people in the Izmyloski Sports Hall in Moscow in 1990.*

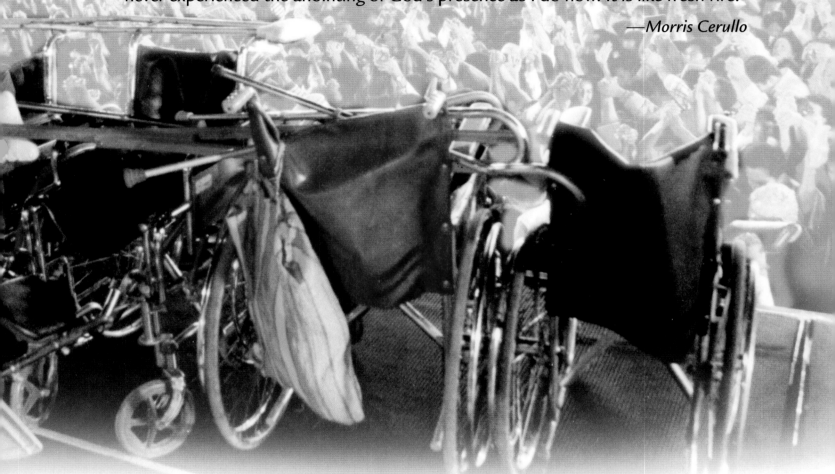

"The glorious vision I received as a young man has remained with me all these years. During times of great adversity, rejection, and persecution it has been a source of strength to me. Knowing God placed His hand upon my life, that He supernaturally called me and promised that His presence would be with me, has kept me focused upon the work He called me to do. I have a greater urgency now than ever. I have never experienced the anointing of God's presence as I do now. It is like fresh fire."

—*Morris Cerullo*

**ON-GOING MINISTRY**
*(above) Abandoned wheelchairs and crutches at a miracle crusade in Guayaquil, Ecuador; 70,000 people attended.*
*(left) Morris and wife, Theresa, have ministered together during fifty-four years of marriage.*

with King Abdullah of Jordan, who pledged his support for the Middle East International Conference. More than twenty-two hundred delegates from seventeen countries experienced a fiery anointing of God's Spirit.

In recognition of his contributions to global evangelization, Cerullo has received honorary doctorates of divinity and humanities. Cerullo has ministered in scores of countries on six continents, sometimes to half a million people at one time. He has personally ministered to heads of state in many nations and has written more than 160 books. Ministering alongside him for fifty-four years has been his wife, Theresa, who serves as the ministry's corporate secretary/treasurer.

Cerullo has pledged to give his remaining strength to reach the unreached and continue to go where the gospel has never been preached.

# PENTECOSTAL PIONEERS

## CHURCH OF GOD

**F**OR NEARLY 120 YEARS, BEGINNING EVEN BEFORE THE AZUSA STREET REVIVAL, THE CHURCH OF GOD HAS MINISTERED THE GOSPEL IN THE POWER OF THE HOLY SPIRIT, AND TODAY HAS A WORLDWIDE MEMBERSHIP OF MORE THAN SEVEN MILLION.

## EARLY OUTPOURING

The Church of God was founded at the foot of the Smoky Mountains on August 19, 1886, when nine believers gathered at a meetinghouse on the banks of Barney Creek in Tennessee, two miles from the North Carolina border. They wanted to start a church full of passion for the high standards of the gospel, spiritual renewal, and Christian unity. The small congregation adopted the name Christian Union, and Baptist minister R. G. Spurling was selected to lead them. He proposed they take the New Testament as their only rule of faith and practice, give each other equal rights to follow their conscience as directed by Scripture and the Holy Spirit, and sit together "as the Church of God."

In 1896, the denomination was forever changed by events taking place a few miles east in Camp Creek, North Carolina. Itinerant evangelists were preaching the doctrine of sanctification in revival services at the Shearer Schoolhouse. During prayer meetings that followed, believers experienced an outpouring

**SHEARER SCHOOLHOUSE (above)**
*An original oil depiction of the Shearer Schoolhouse outpouring is on display at the international offices in Cleveland. The Shearer Schoolhouse outpouring is a pivotal point in Church of God history.*

**NORTH CLEVELAND CHURCH**
*The North Cleveland (TN) Church of God was founded in 1906, the same year of the Azusa Street revival. The next year, evangelist G. B. Cashwell from the Azusa revival would preach there.*

**THE LEADERSHIP AND COMMUNICATIONS CENTER** (top left)
*Located on the international offices campus, it houses a conference center, video production studio and offices for the executive leaders of the denomination.*

**WORLD EVANGELIZATION CENTER** (top right)
*The World Evangelization Center is the anchor of a six building international offices campus. Offices for the denomination have been located in Cleveland, Tennessee, since 1904.*

**INTERNATIONAL OFFICES**
*(left) The World Evangelization Center flanked by the Leadership and Communications Center and Church Ministries Center.*

**EVANGEL**
*The* Evangel *has been the primary publication of the Church of God since 1910.*

of the Holy Spirit accompanied by speaking in tongues and divine healing. On May 15, 1902, this Camp Creek group organized a congregation under the name Holiness Church. Although members of the group had experienced the baptism of the Holy Spirit, they did not yet have a Pentecostal theology.

Missionary evangelist A. J. Tomlinson joined the group a year later and began to plant congregations in Georgia and Tennessee. In January 1906, the Holiness Church decided to come together to "search the Bible for additional light and knowledge." The group gathered for the First General Assembly at Camp Creek. The name "Holiness Church" was changed to "Church of God" at the second assembly in 1907.

## IMPACT

**WORSHIPING TOGETHER**
*Powerful corporate worship and fellowship is the backbone of the Church of God.*

## IMPACT OF AZUSA STREET

The spiritual blessings of the Azusa Street revival reached the Church of God the next year when G. B. Cashwell preached the Pentecostal message to Holiness groups throughout the South. Tomlinson later wrote, "I remember that on the 12th day of January, 1908, while [Brother Cashwell] was standing behind the sacred desk delivering the message[,] the Holy Ghost fell upon this servant of the Lord and after about three hours of wonderful manifestations I knew I had received the Holy Ghost because I spoke in tongues as the Spirit gave utterance."

Tomlinson was elected the Church of God's first general overseer in 1909 and remained in that office until 1923. Under his leadership, the Church of God expanded to several states and in 1909 began its first missions endeavor, to the Bahamas. In 1910, Tomlinson founded a publication, the *Church of God Evangel*. The denomination started Bible Training School (BTS) in 1918 to train workers for ministry and started an orphanage in 1920.

**CARING FOR WIDOWS (top)**
*The Iris B. Vest Widows Care Center offers affordable housing for widows of ministers.*
**CHILDREN'S HOME**
*The administration building of the Smoky Mountain Children's Home is part of the "Care Campus" in Sevierville, Tennessee., which offers benevolent services.*

But in 1923 the Church of God went through a painful financial crisis brought on by a weakened economy and inadequate management. A confrontation between Tomlinson and the Elders Council, which had been created in 1916, led to Tomlinson's removal from office; F. J. Lee succeeded him. The traumatic transition led to the development of what is today called the International Executive Committee. It also set in motion a regular rotation of leadership that is still practiced.

**BAPTIZING BELIEVERS**
*Church of God chaplains work in whatever conditions are available. Here, a new convert is baptized in Afghanistan.*

**ZAMBIA MINISTRY**
*Children from Emma's Kids, a Church of God sponsored home for children, sing at a farm church in Zambia.*

**CHURCH OF GOD IN KOREA**
*Korea and other Asian countries have some of the largest concentrations of Church of God members and are characterized by anointed worship.*

**GLOBAL REACH**
*Church of God sanctuaries come in all shapes and sizes and are in communities at all economic levels.*

## BRANCHING OUT

Over the next decades the Church of God grew in numbers and ministries as its people committed themselves to evangelism at home and abroad. The denomination formed a standing missions board in 1926, a national youth department in 1946, and a national evangelism committee in 1956. The church published Sunday school literature, song books, and other resources under the trade name Pathway Press. The Church of God's regular radio program, *Forward in Faith*, first aired in December 1958.

BTS was renamed Lee College in 1947; it added a liberal arts program in 1968 and achieved university status in 1997. Graduate training began in 1975 with the establishment of what is now the Church of God Theological Seminary. The denomination operates many graduate schools, Bible schools, and training programs outside the United States.

In 2006, the Church of God counts more than 33,000 churches in 166 nations of the world. Many are experiencing the fire of the Holy Spirit today more than ever. Reports of revivals are frequent and ongoing. The denomination has created departments to serve lay ministers, women, musicians, families, and people of all races. In 2004, the Church of God adopted a mission and vision statement committing itself anew to prayer, Pentecostal worship, world evangelization, church planting, leadership development, care, and interdependence.

The Church of God is one of the oldest and most influential global Pentecostal denominations. As it heads into a second century of Pentecost, it relies on the same principles it started with—searching the Scriptures, honoring the consciences of fellow believers, and remaining open to the work of the Holy Spirit. The Church of God will continue to be a channel for Pentecostal revival in the new millennium.

**LEARNING TO SERVE**
*As part of a required curriculum, Lee University students learn the importance of benevolent service.*

**FLAGSHIP UNIVERSITY**
*Lee University in Cleveland, Tennessee, was founded in 1918. More than one hundred Church of God institutions of higher education operate around the world.*

**GENERAL ASSEMBLY**
*Every two years, the Church of God holds a general assembly in a world-class city where the members discuss and vote on issues.*

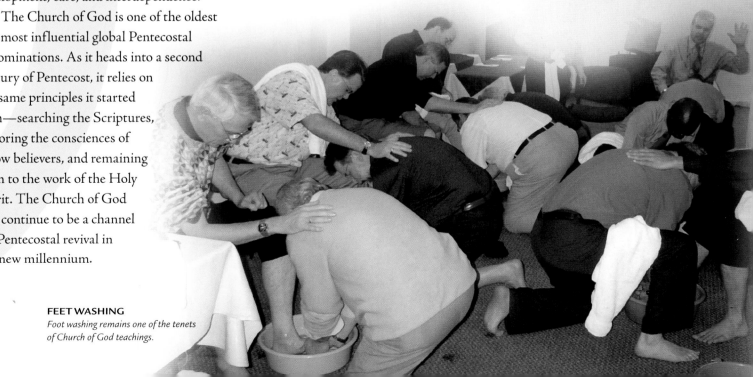

**FEET WASHING**
*Foot washing remains one of the tenets of Church of God teachings.*

# LEGACY AND PROMISE

## CHURCH OF GOD IN CHRIST

**T**HE CHURCH OF GOD IN CHRIST (COGIC), WHICH GREW OUT OF THE AZUSA STREET REVIVAL, IS THE LARGEST PENTECOSTAL DENOMINATION IN THE UNITED STATES AND A PILLAR OF THE PENTECOSTAL MOVEMENT. COGIC IS NOW LED BY PRESIDING BISHOP G. E. PATTERSON.

The denomination's founder, Charles Harrison Mason, was born in 1866 to former slaves near Memphis. As a boy, Charles nearly died of fever, but he was miraculously healed. He was converted in 1878 and baptized by his brother, the pastor of a Missionary Baptist church. In 1893, Charles himself entered the ministry.

Mason was influenced by the Holiness Movement and came to believe in sanctification and perfection characterized by "perfect love." He enrolled at Arkansas Baptist College in 1893 but withdrew after three months, dissatisfied with the teaching. He preached and met Charles Price Jones, the newly elected pastor of a Baptist church in Jackson, Mississippi. Both men preached the doctrine of sanctification at a revival there in 1896, and the teaching caused a breach with the Baptist association, which closed its doors to them. They then joined an informal group known as "the movement" whose members embraced the doctrine of sanctification. Their small congregations bore such names as "Churches of God" and "Churches of Christ."

In 1897, Mason received a revelation concerning the group's name, and the group became the Church of God in Christ. The formalized movement named Jones as general overseer. J. A. Jeter was placed over Arkansas, and Mason was made overseer of Tennessee.

### PENTECOST AND DIVISION

In the fall of 1906 Jones sent Mason, D. J. Young, and Jeter to assess the Azusa Street

COGIC eventually grew from storefronts to megachurches. Today COGIC has eight million members and churches on every continent.

revival they had heard about. Mason later wrote of his experience, "The first day in the meeting I sat to myself, away from those that went with me. I began to thank God in my heart for all things, for when I heard some speak in tongues, I knew it was right though I did not understand it. Nevertheless, it was sweet to me. I also thank God for Elder Seymour who came and preached a wonderful sermon. His words were sweet and powerful."

The second night, Mason had a divine vision that led to his receiving the baptism in the Holy Spirit. Upon returning to Memphis, Mason proclaimed this Pentecostal experience as a New Testament doctrine, but Jeter, Jones, and others regarded the experience as a delusion. The group withdrew its fellowship from Mason, and Mason called a conference in Memphis of all ministers who believed in receiving the baptism of the Holy Ghost. These men organized the first Pentecostal General Assembly of the Church of God in Christ. Mason was chosen unanimously as the general overseer and chief apostle and was given authority to establish doctrine, organize auxiliaries, and appoint overseers.

**G. E. PATTERSON**

## A BROAD REACH

Mason ordained many white ministers from 1909 to 1914 because COGIC was one of the few legally incorporated Pentecostal groups. Scores of white congregations bore the name Church of God in Christ until the prevailing racial and social attitudes of the times caused this to cease. In spite of racial division within the Pentecostal movement, Mason preached for the newly formed Assemblies of God in 1914 and maintained

fellowship with white Pentecostal leaders.

From the start, COGIC churches were musically vibrant, often singing in the tradition of African call and response. Crowds gathered during annual convocations for what amounted to worship concerts. Gospel singers like Sister Rosetta Tharpe, the Clark Sisters, and Andrae Crouch came from COGIC roots.

COGIC eventually grew from storefronts to megachurches. In 1945, Mason dedicated the Mason Temple in Memphis, the largest convention hall owned by any non-white religious group in America at the time. Mason died November 17, 1961. On April 3, 1968, Martin Luther King Jr. delivered his final speech at Mason Temple before being gunned down the next morning.

Today COGIC has eight million members and churches on every continent. It supports missions in fifty-nine countries and operates All Saints Bible College and C. H. Mason Theological Seminary. The denomination has taken strong stances on issues like same-sex marriage and warfare.

COGIC's primary mission remains to carry out the mandate of Jesus Christ as expressed in Matthew 28:19. According to the late Bishop Ithiel Clemmons, the phenomenal growth of COGIC can be traced to a covenant-promise the Lord gave Mason that "the sun would never set upon the expanse of the Church of God in Christ."

*The phenomenal growth of COGIC can be traced to a covenant promise the Lord gave Mason that "the sun would never set upon the expanse of the Church of God in Christ."*

# A JOURNEY OF FAITH
## KENNETH COPELAND MINISTRIES

**MINISTERING TOGETHER**
*Kenneth and Gloria share a special moment at a Kenneth Copeland Ministries meeting.*

**HEADQUARTERS**
*Kenneth Copeland Ministries headquarters building, Fort Worth, Texas.*

**K**ENNETH COPELAND LEFT A CAREER AS A CHART-TOPPING POP SINGER AND LATER BECAME ONE OF THE LEADING FAITH TEACHERS OF THE PAST THIRTY-NINE YEARS. HIS TELEVISION PROGRAM, *BELIEVER'S VOICE OF VICTORY*, BROADCASTS WORLDWIDE, AND HE AND HIS WIFE, GLORIA, ARE WELL-KNOWN CONFERENCE SPEAKERS AND AUTHORS.

Copeland grew up in a Christian household with a praying mother, but he left the church and pursued a singing career that peaked in 1957 when his song "Pledge of Love" entered the top ten and sold 300,000 copies. His music career was cut short when the U.S. Army drafted him. After leaving the military he became a commercial pilot and entered into several business ventures, all of which failed. He said later that he was running from a call to preach he had received years earlier.

## TURNAROUND

In 1962, Ken and Gloria met Christ and were baptized in the Holy Spirit. In 1966, still financially broke, Ken enrolled at Oral Roberts University and became Roberts' personal pilot. Through the example and teaching of Roberts and Kenneth E. Hagin Sr., the Copelands embraced the message of faith and healing. In 1967, while praying in a dry riverbed in Tulsa, Copeland says God commissioned him into ministry.

"I hadn't known God long enough back then to understand that He always thinks big," Copeland later wrote. "He told me exactly what He was calling me to do. He was calling me to preach the gospel to the nations.... There I was, as poor as a field mouse, driving an old Oldsmobile in need of a miracle, living in a little rented house—and I was called to the nations. He said things that I had no idea how I would ever be able to do, but I said yes to it all. I began meditating on what He said."

The Copelands set strict rules for their ministry: they would not ask for a place to preach, and they would never preach based on a financial arrangement. Soon Ken was holding faith seminars and revivals, but crowds remained small for the first decade. He decided that no matter how many people showed up, he would preach the same way.

## ABUNDANCE

In the 1970s Copeland's tape and radio ministries began to flourish. He initially made

"I'm consumed by the fact that Jesus is Lord. Someday everyone, Christian or not, will bow their knee and confess that He is Lord. Why wait? Every day, in every way, I want to say to Him, 'Jesus, You are my Lord!'"

—Kenneth Copeland

**IN PRAYER**
Kenneth prays during a Kenneth Copeland Ministries meeting.

**PRINCIPLES OF FAITH**

*(top) Gloria prays the prayer of faith during Healing School.*

*(bottom) Gloria preaches at a Kenneth Copeland Ministries meeting.*

copies of reel-to-reel tapes on his own, one at a time, sometimes staying up all night. But demand rose, and, with the help of a tape duplicator, he began selling and giving away thousands of tapes that went around the world.

Copeland's first venture into radio failed, but the following year his radio program became the fastest-growing religious broadcast in radio history. He ended the year on seven hundred stations.

In 1978 the Copelands began holding weeklong conventions instead of two- or three-day meetings, so people could be "totally immersed in the Word of God." The format proved popular around the world. Their traveling ministry, which began with a single station wagon, soon required six 18-wheelers and a traveling staff of fifty. At the meetings many people were healed, encouraged, and saved. Speakers included preachers like Fred Price, Creflo Dollar, Oral Roberts, Charles Capps, T. L. Osborn, and Kenneth Hagin Sr.

The Copelands began their weekly television ministry in 1979 with the *Believer's Voice of Victory* and have been on the air ever since, now broadcasting to the world six times a week on nearly five hundred stations. In 1986 they built a ministry headquarters at Eagle Mountain Lake in Newark, Texas, near Fort Worth. Ken and Gloria have written more than sixty books. Their *Believer's Voice of Victory* and *Shout!* magazines go to nearly seven hundred thousand people.

The Copelands are among the most active, recognized, and sought-after ministry speakers in the country. They have led countless believers on a journey to maturity in the principles of faith, love, healing, prosperity, redemption, and righteousness. They teach that every Christian can conquer every problem and challenge by faith. The Copelands continue to pursue the goal they set thirty-nine years ago, "to proclaim that Jesus is Lord from the top of the world to the bottom and all the way around."

Kenneth Copeland Ministries' prison outreach reaches 60,000 prisoners a year. KCM processes 30,000 pieces of incoming mail from inmates each month.

*AT HOME*
*Kenneth and Gloria Copeland.*

**ON-SITE CHURCH**
*Eagle Mountain International Church on the*
*grounds of Kenneth Copeland Ministries.*
*The church is pastored by George and Terri*
*Copeland Pearsons.*

# TULSA'S EVANGELISM POWERHOUSE

## BILLY JOE AND SHARON DAUGHERTY, VICTORY CHRISTIAN CENTER

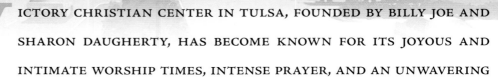

V ICTORY CHRISTIAN CENTER IN TULSA, FOUNDED BY BILLY JOE AND SHARON DAUGHERTY, HAS BECOME KNOWN FOR ITS JOYOUS AND INTIMATE WORSHIP TIMES, INTENSE PRAYER, AND AN UNWAVERING COMMITMENT TO TAKING THE GOSPEL LOCALLY AND TO THE WORLD. IN 2006, THE CHURCH MOVES INTO A NEW FIVE-THOUSAND-SEAT SANCTUARY.

From the first service in 1981, the Daughertys committed themselves to building an interdenominational and multiracial church. The congregation met in a car dealership, a junior high school, and in the Oral Roberts University (ORU) Mabee Center. Additional services were added in the newly constructed facility across the street from ORU in 1996.

The church aggressively pursued its fivefold vision of worship, prayer, the Word of God, fellowship, and evangelism. Through the words of 2 Timothy 2:2 ("And the things that you have heard from me among many witnesses, commit these to faithful men who will be able teach others also"), God spoke to them to start

Victory Bible Institute. The ministry set a goal of placing missionaries in every nation. Today Victory Bible Institute operates 232 International Victory Bible Institutes in 56 countries.

The church also launched missions at home, founding the Tulsa Dream Center in a thirty-thousand-square-foot facility on eighty acres next to what was the most crime-ridden area in Tulsa. The Dream Center offers a medical and dental clinic, legal services, recreation programs, computer training, food, clothing, and ministry for all age groups. In the past few years the Dream Center has helped bring the crime rate down in that part of the city.

**TRAINING GENERATIONS**
*(right) The Victory Bible Institute building also houses the Victory Missions Department and is used for Saturday Bus Ministry and Hispanic Ministry. (far right) International Victory Bible Institute students in the Philippines.*

**WHERE DREAMS COME TRUE**
*At the Tulsa Dream Center, people find wholeness and healing as people care for and pray with them.*

**24.7 YOUTH AND 3D YOUNG ADULTS**
*Victory's youth programs help young people find their purpose in life through cell groups, teen mission trips, and personal ministry.*

## A VIBRANT CHURCH COMMUNITY

Victory's ministries have diversified to meet many needs. Each week Victory buses hundreds of people to church, and from March to October Mobile Kidz trucks take evangelism ministry into the neighborhoods. The 24.7 Youth and 3D ministries reach teens and young adults in a café and music setting. Camp Victory, a beautiful parklike property outside of Tulsa, hosts year-round teaching, prayer, missions training, and summer camps for children from all economic situations.

Victory Christian School, a fully accredited K–12 school, trains thirteen-hundred-plus students a year with high-quality academics, sports, music, drama, computers, missions, and art. The school is on the cutting edge of educational innovation while teaching young people Christ-centered values.

Victory Christian Center's ministries continue to grow and flourish, reaching to the ends of the earth through television and radio, printed materials, and crusades and outreaches in many nations of the world. (See www.victory.com.) Pastors Billy Joe and Sharon have followed the leading of the Holy Spirit to create a unique church community that is alive and active with love for the Lord.

**CAMP VICTORY**
*On a parklike property outside of Tulsa, Camp Victory offers year-round ministry events and camps for children of all economic backgrounds.*

**DAUGHERTY FAMILY**
*(left) Billy Joe and wife, Sharon, minister God's healing, saving, and delivering power as a team. Their four children and sons-in-law work alongside them in the ministry.*

# DAYSTAR RISING
## DAYSTAR TELEVISION

**I**N TWENTY-ONE YEARS, DAYSTAR TELEVISION HAS BECOME THE FASTEST-GROWING, SECOND-LARGEST CHRISTIAN TELEVISION NETWORK IN THE WORLD. BY APPEALING TO A WIDE SPECTRUM OF VIEWERS ACROSS GENERATIONAL, CULTURAL, AND DENOMINATIONAL LINES, DAYSTAR HAS BECOME THE DESTINATION CHANNEL FOR A GROWING NUMBER OF CHRISTIAN VIEWERS TODAY DAYSTAR OWNS STATIONS IN ALL MAJOR U.S. MARKETS AND BROADCASTS TO THE WORLD VIA SATELLITE.

### BUILDING THE DREAM

Daystar founder Marcus Lamb of Macon, Georgia, began preaching at fifteen, and four years later graduated magna cum laude from Lee College. He met Joni Trammell while preaching revival services in Greenville, South Carolina. In 1982, they married and began ministering together.

In 1983, Marcus wrestled with the question of how to reach the most people with the gospel. While visiting the Holy Land and standing on the Mount of Olives, God called him to build Christian television stations, he says. When the license for an Alabama television station became available, the Lambs moved to Montgomery to build WMCF-TV Channel 45. Before the station's license expired they had to raise money, build the station with their own hands, and go on the air, or they would forfeit the license and lose everything they had invested.

Few people contributed to the cause, but the Lambs leveraged most of what they and their parents owned. In 1985, seven days before their first child was born, WMCF-TV Channel 45 went on the air, the first full-power Christian television station in the state. The Lambs put together a talk-show format and learned in front of the camera. At twenty-seven, Marcus was the youngest person to build a television station in the United States.

**MOVING UP**
*(below, left to right) In 1993, the Lambs' KMPX-TV 29 hit the airwaves in Dallas/Fort Worth, a market of more than four million people. Their potential audience was significantly larger than in their previous market in Montgomery, Alabama. The KMPX-TV 29 master control room transmitter site. A "45 Alive" Shar-a-thon at station WMCF-TV 45 in Montgomery, Alabama.*

**MINISTRY HEADQUARTERS**

*(left) The present Daystar Television Network headquarters in the greater Dallas/ Fort Worth Metroplex, a 90,000-square-feet facility. (below, left to right) The Lambs in the opening view of the former* Celebration *program at KMPX-TV 29 studio in Dallas/Ft. Worth. The Lambs during Shar-a-thon "Harvest 95" at KMPX-TV 29.*

## A GROWING AUDIENCE

In 1990, the Lambs moved to Dallas to build a new Christian television station and minister to a potentially much larger audience. They purchased a single UHF television station in the Dallas-Ft. Worth Metroplex, KMPX-TV Channel 29. The Lambs had little money to fund the effort, but they benefited from deregulation in the television market, which made independent channels across the nation available for purchase. Major networks were

limited to owning only seven stations. "Must carry" rules required cable TV companies to carry local stations, giving them the same access to viewers that major networks enjoyed.

Through a series of miracles, KMPX-TV Channel 29 hit the airwaves in 1993, eventually reaching four million people. The Lambs scooped up another UHF station in Macon, Georgia, and an educational station in Denver. The three stations became the fledgling Daystar Television Network.

In August 1997, the ministry moved into a new thirty-two-thousand-square-foot studio facility. The Daystar Television Network was

**THE WAY IT WAS**

*The former* Celebration *program interview set at KMPX-TV 29.*

**IN TOUCH**
*Daystar's international prayer
ministry includes sixty-four
prayer partners and an international team that faithfully
ministers to viewers around
the world twenty-four hours
a day, seven days a week.*

officially launched on New Year's Eve 1997 with a broadcast featuring T. D. Jakes from The Potter's House.

In 2000, the FCC cleared the way for round-the-clock religious programming on educational television stations, whose licenses were less expensive. The Lambs acquired educational

stations in Houston, Seattle, Phoenix, Boston, Little Rock, and Honolulu as donations flowed in. By 2002, Daystar owned nineteen television stations. That year Daystar debuted on DIRECTV, then on the Dish Network.

In 2003, Daystar acquired KDTN-TV Channel 2 and became the only Christian television network in the United States to own a VHF station in a major market. That same year, Daystar moved into the International Ministry Center, a ninety-thousand-square-foot corporate headquarters building that included two state-of-the-art production studios.

## REACHING THE WORLD

Through faith and perseverance, Daystar has emerged as one of the leading Christian networks in the history of television. Daystar now owns and/or operates forty-five television stations in the top thirty U.S. markets. It can

**CUTTING EDGE**
*(below) The high-tech, contemporary* Celebration *set is unlike that of any other Christian talk show's.*

**CELEBRATION SET**
*Inside the production studio of the* Celebration *interview set.*

be seen on worldwide satellite television, cable systems, and the Internet at www.daystar.com. Daystar reaches fifty million households in the United States with a message of faith, hope, and salvation, and broadcasts to the entire globe.

Daystar now employs nearly three hundred people and operates production facilities in Dallas, Houston, Denver, Atlanta, and Kentucky. The centerpiece of Daystar's ministry is the Prayer Department, which fields calls around the clock. Daystar also offers a diverse lineup of programming, including *Celebration*, an hour-long talk show hosted by the Lambs and featuring a live band and interviews with leaders and artists like CeCe Winans, John Tesh, George Foreman, Phil Driscoll, Kirk Cameron, Kathy Lee Gifford, and Deion Sanders. *Joni*, a daily half-hour talk show hosted by Joni Lamb, was given the Best Talk Show of the Year award by the National Religious Broadcasters in 2004.

Daystar is the leading provider of "live" remote broadcasts of major Christian events, allowing viewers to participate in today's most popular Christian conferences, concerts, camp meetings, and revivals. Daystar airs programs by Joel Osteen, Bishop T. D. Jakes,

Joyce Meyer, Charles Stanley, Kenneth and Gloria Copeland, Benny Hinn, Jesse Duplantis, Ed Young, Gaither Homecoming, Reinhard Bonnke, and Hillsong. Daystar offers Spanish viewers *Celebracion en Daystar*, a talk show, and the network plans to devote a digital channel exclusively to Spanish-language content. Daystar is also pioneering programs for children and teens.

Marcus and Joni Lamb are confident that their mainstream personal style and Christian beliefs will continue to draw a wide spectrum of viewers. The destiny of Daystar remains squarely in God's hands as He uses it to take the gospel around the world.

**LAMB FAMILY**
*Marcus and Joni Lamb with children Rachel (left), Jonathan, and Rebecca.*

# ALL THE GOSPEL TO ALL THE WORLD

## JOHN HAGEE MINISTRIES

**FRIEND OF ISRAEL**
*Hagee is a strong supporter of solidarity between Christians and Jews. He has deep ties with the State of Israel and the Jewish people.*
*T-B: Hagee with Prime Minister Menachem Begin; with Prime Minister Yitzak Rabin; with Prime Minister Benjamin Netanyahu.*

**J**OHN C. HAGEE, FOUNDER AND SENIOR PASTOR OF CORNERSTONE CHURCH IN SAN ANTONIO, TEXAS, HAS BUILT A MINISTRY ON STRAIGHTFORWARD BIBLE TEACHING, IN-DEPTH STUDY OF END-TIME EVENTS, AND UNWAVERING SUPPORT FOR THE NATION OF ISRAEL AND THE JEWISH PEOPLE.

### THE MAN

John Hagee is a fifth-generation pastor and the forty-seventh descendent of his family to preach the gospel since they immigrated to America from Germany. Hagee received his bachelor's degree from Trinity University, earned a master's degree from North Texas University, and trained in theology at Southwestern Bible Institute. After completing his education, he settled in San Antonio where he built four separate sanctuary and education complexes.

Hagee married Diana Castro, and together they raised five children while pastoring their beloved eighteen-thousand-member Cornerstone Church founded by Hagee in 1975.

### THE MINISTRY

While pastoring the evangelical, non-denominational Cornerstone Church, Hagee acquired licenses for two low-power television stations in San Antonio over twenty-eight years ago. The Cornerstone family sacrificially gave to buy the necessary broadcasting equipment with the Hagees personally mortgaging their home to help build the radio and television ministry. Hagee negotiated with a national cable provider allowing him to locally broadcast Christian programming twenty-four hours a day, seven days a week.

Today, John Hagee Ministries occupies a 50,000 square-foot production center that houses both radio and television studios, 100 telephone prayer partners, and a vast distribution center. Currently, Hagee telecasts on 8 major networks, 162 independent television stations, and 51 radio stations throughout the globe broadcasting in more than 120 nations.

**MINISTRY HEADQUARTERS**
*The John Hagee International Media Center today—a 50,000-square-foot facility housing a staff of more than 120.*

**HAGEE FAMILY**
*John and Diana Hagee have five married children and five granddaughters, with their sixth grandbaby on the way.*

In addition to founding the global media ministry, Hagee is the author of twenty-one major books, the latest being *Jerusalem Countdown*. Many of his books have been best sellers, with one, *The Beginning of the End*, reaching the *New York Times* best-sellers list.

An accomplished singer and musician, Hagee and his children have also produced four southern gospel musical projects. He has been awarded honorary doctorates by Oral Roberts University, Canada Christian College, and Netanya Academic College of Israel.

Hagee is the founder of "A Night to Honor Israel," which is celebrated annually at Cornerstone Church and over national and international television. Hagee has been presented the ZOA Israel Award, the ZOA Service Award, and the Humanitarian of the Year Award by the B'Nai B'Rith Council in recognition of his unwavering support of Israel.

Hagee's ministry has given millions of dollars to bring the Jewish exiles of the world home to Israel. The ministry has provided comfort and consolation to the Jewish people through the building of orphanage facilities, absorption centers, and hospitals.

## THE MISSION

John Hagee penned his mission and purpose in 1991, and it reads… *To build a television ministry for the purpose of evangelizing America and the world. To pastor a New Testament church filled with signs and wonders that will bless the city of San Antonio and receive the nations of the world to restore, unite, train, and teach the lost, the brokenhearted, and the discouraged, and heal the sick and provide deliverance to the oppressed—all of this to be done to the glory of God the Father and His Son Jesus through the power of the Holy Spirit.*

**SIXTH GENERATION**
*Matthew Hagee is following in his father's footsteps with a passion to preach the gospel and has accepted the mantle to continue the Hagee family legacy.*

**BEST-SELLING AUTHOR**
*Hagee is an author of twenty-one major books, his newest release being* Jerusalem Countdown.

# JACK HAYFORD

# BRIDGE BUILDER

**J**ACK HAYFORD IS BEST KNOWN AS THE FOUNDING PASTOR OF THE CHURCH ON THE WAY IN VAN NUYS, CALIFORNIA, WHICH GREW FROM EIGHTEEN MEMBERS TO TEN THOUSAND MEMBERS IN THREE DECADES UNDER HIS LEADERSHIP. IN FIFTY YEARS OF MINISTRY AS AN IN-TERNATIONAL SPEAKER, MUSICAL COMPOSER, AND DENOMINATIONAL LEADER, HAYFORD HAS EMBODIED INTEGRITY AND SERVED THE BODY OF CHRIST AS A PASTOR TO PASTORS, TRAINING UP GENERATIONS OF SPIRIT-FILLED LEADERS. TODAY HE IS ONE OF THE MOST WIDELY KNOWN AND RESPECTED PENTECOSTAL LEADERS IN THE WORLD.

Jack Hayford was born in Los Angeles and married Anna Smith, whom he met while both were attending L.I.F.E. Bible College in Los Angeles. They moved to Ft. Wayne, Indiana, to plant a Foursquare church. After four years of experiencing the learning processes and trials of every young couple in ministry, a small work was planted. By reason of youth ministry involvements simultaneous with the church plant, Jack and Anna were asked to assume the national youth leadership of the Foursquare movement (1960–1965). The following five years

**LEADERSHIP PRIORITIES**
*Worship and intercession were established as early priorities, even from the days at the original Van Nuys chapel.*

**MARRIAGE**
*(left) The Hayfords at their entry into pastoral ministry, their wedding, and their fiftieth wedding anniversary.*

Jack served as a faculty member and executive administrator at his alma mater.

In 1969, the Hayfords accepted the interim pastorate of an eighteen-member Foursquare church in Van Nuys. After six months, the Lord spoke to him, directing him to stay, saying, "You mustn't think too small, or you'll get in My way."

## A NATIONAL PROFILE

Named The Church On The Way by reason of its location on a major thoroughfare, and focused on worship and the teaching of the Word of God, growth began to abound. Hayford's television ministry began in 1977 and expanded to radio in 1981. His balanced,

**SHAPING LEADERS**
*(top to bottom) Hayford mentoring at the School of Pastoral Nurture; seen also at The King's commencement with Scott Bauer (2003).*

biblical teaching soon found an international audience, and he was invited to speak at the Lausanne II Congress on World Evangelism, the Pentecostal World Conference, National Religious Broadcasters conventions, the Gospel Music Association, the Billy Graham Evangelistic Association's Schools of Evangelism, and the National Prayer Service following the inaugural ceremonies for President George W. Bush. He also spoke regularly at Promise Keepers events across the nation and anchored the organization's 1997 Stand in the Gap event on the Mall in Washington DC.

Hayford's passionate yet nontheatrical style and biblically based, Spirit-filled teaching continue to earn him the respect of Christians across the doctrinal spectrum. He is editorial advisor for *Ministries Today* and Christianity Today's *Leadership Journal* and general editor of the Spirit-Filled Life publications published by Thomas Nelson Publishers. That series has sold more than two million volumes. He has been a guest on Ted Koppel's *Prime Time Special*, ABC's *Prime Time*, the USA Radio Network, Christian Broadcasting Network, Focus on the Family, Moody Broadcasting, and *The Merv Griffin Show*.

Hayford is a prolific writer of books, hymns, and choruses. His best-known song is "Majesty."

**"THE SECRET OF MY SUCCESS"**
*With a smile, Hayford often affirms the strength, support, and a near-lifetime gift of God he has received in his wife, Anna. "Her partnership and the absolute mutuality we share in life and vision are central to any fruitfulness God has granted me." (right) The Hayfords with their children and grandchildren, Christmas 2002.*

**MINISTRY SCOPE AND INFLUENCE**
*Representative of the breadth of Hayford's service over 50 years: (left to right) 1. With Billy Graham, serving as a co-chairman in the greater Los Angeles crusade. 2. With David Cho, ministering at Full Gospel Central Church, Seoul. 3. With Fred Price, Ken Ulmer, and Lloyd Ogilvie, leading the interdenominational prayer gatherings for the L.A.-area pastors. 4. In Jerusalem as a guest of Israel's prime minister, Ariel Sharon.*

Today Hayford serves as chancellor of The King's College, which he founded in 1987, and The King's Seminary, which he founded in 1997. Through his School of Pastoral Nurture, each month he welcomes and mentors 45 different pastors during weeklong intensives with sessions held at the seminary in his home. Hayford also serves as president of the International Church of the Foursquare Gospel, which has a constituency of more than 5 million, with 49,000 churches in 146 nations. His television program, *Spirit Formed*, can be seen across North America.

**MEDIA MINISTRY**
*Through thirty years of radio, twenty-five years of television and more than fifty books, five hundred songs, and millions of tapes, Hayford's teaching has reached out to the world.*

Hayford continues to model biblical and personal integrity as a bridge builder in the body of Christ.

# AN INSTRUMENT OF HOLINESS

## INTERNATIONAL PENTECOSTAL HOLINESS CHURCH

**F**OR MORE THAN ONE HUNDRED YEARS, THE INTERNATIONAL PENTECOSTAL HOLINESS CHURCH (IPHC) AND ITS PREDECESSOR ORGANIZATIONS HAVE CARRIED OUT THE GREAT COMMISSION IN THE POWER OF THE HOLY SPIRIT. FROM ITS REBIRTH AS A RESULT OF THE AZUSA STREET REVIVAL, TO THE HEALING REVIVALS OF THE 1950S, TO THE RECENT EMPHASIS ON PRAYER AND EVANGELISM, THE IPHC HAS LED THE PENTECOSTAL MOVEMENT AT KEY MOMENTS IN ITS HISTORY.

### "OPENING THE WINDOWS OF HEAVEN"

The IPHC was born in January 1911 when two Holiness denominations merged after each was profoundly transformed by the Azusa Street Revival. The Fire-Baptized Holiness Church had been formed in 1898 and had spread across the U.S. Midwest, South, and Canada. A leadership crisis in 1900 almost disintegrated the organization, but through the efforts of J. H. King, a former Methodist preacher from Georgia, the movement survived and grew.

The Pentecostal Holiness Church of North Carolina, which dropped the word "Pentecostal" from its name between 1901 and 1909, had been established in 1898 through the ministry of former Methodist evangelist A. B. Crumpler. In November 1906, Gaston B. Cashwell, a white evangelist with the denomination, visited Azusa Street, and his experience brought major changes to southern Holiness churches.

**IPHC LEADERS**
*(top left) Bishop Joseph H. King, formerly a Methodist minister, received Pentecost under the ministry of G. B. Cashwell. King was the first general superintendent of the International Pentecostal Holiness Church.*
*(below left) James D. Leggett, presiding bishop, has led the IPHC since 1997. During his tenure, the church has experienced its most significant growth.*
*(right) The merger between the Fire Baptized Holiness Church and the Pentecostal Holiness Church of North Carolina took place in 1911 in the Octagon Tabernacle in Falcon, North Carolina.*

At Azusa Street, Cashwell confronted his racial prejudice and asked William Seymour to lay hands on him and pray that he would receive the baptism with the Holy Spirit. Cashwell wrote in *The Apostolic Faith* (December 1906), "The first altar call I went forward in earnest for my Pentecost. I struggled from Sunday till Thursday. While seeking in an upstairs room in the mission, the Lord opened up the windows of heaven and the light of God began to flow over me in such power as never before. I then went into the room where the service was held, and while Sister Lum was reading of how the

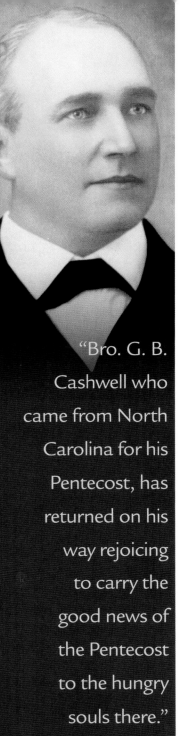

"Bro. G. B. Cashwell who came from North Carolina for his Pentecost, has returned on his way rejoicing to carry the good news of the Pentecost to the hungry souls there."

—William Seymour

Holy Ghost was falling in other places, before I knew it, I began to speak in tongues and praise God. A brother interpreted some of the words to be, 'I love God with all my soul.' He filled me with His Spirit and love, and I am now feasting and drinking at the fountain continually and speak as the Spirit gives utterance, both in my own language and in the unknown language."

Seymour announced in *The Apostolic Faith* that "Bro. G. B. Cashwell who came from North Carolina for his Pentecost, has returned on his way rejoicing to carry the good news of the Pentecost to the hungry souls there."

## NEW BEGINNINGS

Back in Dunn, North Carolina, Cashwell led a revival from December 31, 1906, through mid-January 1907, with long-term effects. In two years Cashwell led hundreds into Pentecost, including J. H. King, M. M. Pinson, who later became one of the first executive presbyters of the Assemblies of God, A. J. Tomlinson, who founded the Church of God (Cleveland, Tennessee), and N. J. Holmes of Greenville, South Carolina.

As a result of Cashwell's revival, the Holiness Church of North Carolina and the

Fire-Baptized Holiness Church, who shared common theologies and vision, merged in Falcon, North Carolina, on January 31, 1911, to form the Pentecostal Holiness Church. "International" was added in the 1970s to reflect the worldwide impact of the church. The denominations' common beliefs, influenced by Seymour's theology, included belief in sanctification as a second definite work of grace, the baptism with the Holy Spirit as a separate work from sanctification and with speaking in tongues as its initial evidence, and divine healing.

In 1921, a split within the IPHC led to the formation of the Congregational Holiness Church, a sister Pentecostal denomination.

Over the next few decades, the IPHC consolidated its theology and expanded to other parts of the United States. In the 1950s the IPHC joined the National Association of Evangelicals and became a founding member of the Pentecostal and Charismatic Churches of North America. In that same decade the IPHC was profoundly affected by the

**WORLDWIDE EFFORT**
*(below) The 5,000-member Redemption World Outreach Center, Greenville, South Carolina, is the largest Pentecostal Holiness Church in the United States.*
*(right) Missionary Joe Arthur conducts an outdoor service in Africa, one of the fastest growing fields for the IPHC.*
*(below right) At the 2003 Youth Quest in Chattanooga, Tennessee, young people commit themselves to intercessory prayer. As a result TWIN (Teen World Intercession Network) was formed.*

> "...become a kingdom of worshiping priests who will worship Him with all their... spirit, soul, and body."
>
> —*The Jerusalem Procalmation*

healing ministry of Oral Roberts and the accompanying wave of revival that preceded the Charismatic movement in the 1960s and 1970s. In the 1970s the denominational headquarters was moved to Oklahoma City from Franklin Springs, Georgia.

In the 1980s the IPHC established the World Intercession Network (WIN), a denomination-wide intercessory prayer movement, to help it reach the world through accelerated evangelism. It also began a concerted effort to plant strong churches, especially in urban centers.

The First World Conference of Pentecostal Holiness Churches, meeting in Jerusalem in 1990, helped to produce the prophetic "Jerusalem Proclamation," in which the IPHC called churches to worship and global missions. At a 1996 Solemn Assembly in Fayetteville, North Carolina, hundreds of leaders repented of corporate sins including a controlling spirit, the elder brother syndrome, greed, judgmentalism, male domination, racism, and spiritual pride.

In the 1990s the denomination shifted from a "hierarchical" to a "networking" model

**RECONCILIATION**
*The late Bishop B. E. Underwood, former general superintendent of the IPHC, was instrumental in planning the "Memphis Miracle." At that meeting, the Pentecostal Fellowship of North America (PFNA), an all-white, traditional Pentecostal association, was dissolved, and the more inclusive Pentecostal-Charismatic Churches of North America (PCCNA) was formed.*

**IPHC WORLDWIDE**

*Examples of the movement's global influence can be seen in the Kopporu Church in India (top left) and a growing congregation in a village in the Ukraine (top right). Though the Ukrainian church was constructed to seat 400, about 650 worshipers attend the services regularly.*

of governmental relationships. In the 2000s the IPHC accepted that the full range of leadership gifts in Ephesians 4:11 operates in the church.

## CONTINUED EXPANSION

Today the IPHC has 290,000 U.S. adherents and 2,020 local congregations, mostly in the Southeast and Midwest. The largest U.S. congregation is the 6,000-member Redemption World Outreach Center in Greenville, South Carolina, led by Ron Carpenter Jr. There are 11,400 IPHC congregations and 1.3 million members overseas, and affiliations with like-faith churches place the total worldwide membership at more than 3.7 million.

The IPHC operates several college-level educational institutions, including Emmanuel College in Franklin Springs, Georgia, and Southwestern Christian University and Graduate School in Bethany, Oklahoma. It operates twenty-five training institutes overseas.

The IPHC was birthed in the missionary impulse of Azusa Street and is poised to serve as an instrument of grace, holiness, and power for the next one hundred years.

**TRAINING GENERATIONS**

*(below right) The Wing Kwong Church in Hong Kong is the largest Pentecostal Holiness Church in the world with more than 6,000 members. The church's Junior Lifeliner program reaches 5,000 teenagers weekly. The IPHC operates several college-level institutions, including Emmanuel College (below left) in Franklin Springs, Georgia, and Southwestern Christian University and Graduate School in Bethany, Oklahoma.*

# COVERING THE EARTH WITH THE WORD

## MARILYN HICKEY MINISTRIES

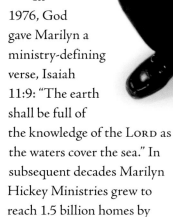

**M**ARILYN HICKEY HAS BUILT ONE OF THE MOST RESPECTED BIBLE TEACHING AND EVANGELISM MINISTRIES OF THE PAST THREE DECADES. FOLLOWING HER GOD-GIVEN MANDATE TO "COVER THE EARTH WITH GOD'S WORD," HICKEY HAS MINISTERED IN MORE THAN ONE HUNDRED NATIONS, COFOUNDED A LEADING CHARISMATIC CHURCH IN DENVER, AND CONTINUED HOSTING A DAILY TELEVISION SHOW. NOW JOINED IN MINISTRY BY DAUGHTER SARAH BOWLING, HICKEY IS TAKING SPIRIT-EMPOWERED BIBLE TEACHING AROUND THE WORLD.

## SHOEBOX BEGINNINGS

As a girl, Marilyn had little time for spiritual things, even after her mother committed her life to Christ and received the baptism in the Holy Spirit. Marilyn became a public school teacher and met Wallace Hickey, a Spirit-filled man who brought her back to church and to the Lord. They married in 1954, but doctors said Marilyn would never bear a child. In 1958, evangelist William Branham prophesied that Marilyn would conceive. Ten years later, Sarah was born.

The Hickeys founded Orchard Road Christian Center (ORCC) with twenty-five people in Denver in 1960. Marilyn started a home Bible study that quickly multiplied to twenty-two groups. Soon she was teaching on radio and television, initially supported by her home Bible study attendees. Viewers and listeners wrote to say they were blessed by Marilyn's fresh, practical approach to the Bible. The ministry began with a single volunteer, Marilyn's mother, and a shoebox full of mail on the kitchen table.

In 1976, God gave Marilyn a ministry-defining verse, Isaiah 11:9: "The earth shall be full of the knowledge of the LORD as the waters cover the sea." In subsequent decades Marilyn Hickey Ministries grew to reach 1.5 billion homes by television. Hickey conducted crusades, including in the heart of the Muslim world, spoke widely in conferences, and published dozens of books, CDs, and videos. The heart of her ministry lies in the power of God's Word to change lives.

More than two decades ago, Marilyn established a Bible school, now known as Word

**STARTING OUT**
(top to bottom) Marilyn Hickey Ministries began at the Hickeys' kitchen table. Marilyn's mother was the first ministry volunteer and answered mail they received from listeners and viewers. Marilyn's first media outreach was a five-minute radio program, supported initially by the members of her Denver-area Bible studies.

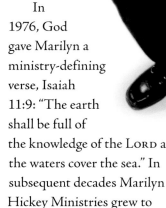

**ON THE AIR**
Marilyn Hickey and daughter Sarah Bowling on the set of their international television program. The broadcast reaches potentially 1.5 billion households.

to the World. Today the school has four sister schools overseas and four more are planned. Seventy percent of its graduates are in active ministry.

Recently, Hickey has been the guest of international leaders, including the president of Ethiopia, officials in Pakistan, and the wife of late Egyptian leader Anwar Sadat. This was prophesied decades ago by Daisy Osborne, wife of evangelist T. L. Osborne, though at the time Marilyn thought the idea far-fetched.

Hickey has also served as chairperson of the board of regents of Oral Roberts University and on the board of directors for David Yonggi Cho's Church Growth International. Her telephone prayer center has ministered to as many as half a million callers annually.

**BEYOND BORDERS**
*Marilyn preaches with passion in Pakistan and meets with King Abdullah II of Jordan.*

carry the legacy of Marilyn Hickey Ministries has run deep since her profound encounter with God in 1993. Mother and daughter continue to carry the gospel into scores of nations, and Sarah teaches with a style distinctly her own. God has shown Marilyn that through Sarah the ministry He ordained will continue in the decades to come.

Inspired by George Otis' Transformation video series, ORCC has spearheaded city prayer, a prayer campaign for the city of Denver. In the near future, Marilyn and Sarah plan to host women's conferences around North and South America; return to Pakistan, Algeria, China, and Morocco for ministry; and create new Bible reading plans to draw young people deeper into God's Word.

Marilyn Hickey is fond of saying, "Make no small plans." From the days of the shoebox full of letters to today's worldwide influence, Marilyn and Sarah believe the best is yet to come.

## NO SMALL PLANS

Today, Marilyn, daughter Sarah, and their husbands co-pastor ORCC. Sarah's passion to

**A FRESH WORD**
*At a meeting in Panama, thousands receive Christ after hearing Sarah preach the gospel. God has shown Marilyn that through Sarah, the ministry will continue for decades to come.*

The heart of her ministry lies in the power of GOD'S WORD to change lives.

# REAL VICTORY

JOYCE MEYER MINISTRIES

**J**OYCE MEYER EMERGED FROM A LIFE OF PAINFUL EXPERIENCES TO BECOME ONE OF THE MOST RECOGNIZED AND RESPECTED BIBLE TEACHERS IN AMERICA. HER *ENJOYING EVERYDAY LIFE* BROADCAST CAN BE SEEN BY TWO-THIRDS OF THE GLOBE. HER BEST-SELLING BOOKS AND DOWN-TO-EARTH TEACHING STYLE HAVE HELPED MILLIONS OF PEOPLE FIND VICTORY IN EVERYDAY LIFE THROUGH THE POWER OF JESUS CHRIST.

As a child, Meyer suffered years of sexual, verbal, and emotional abuse. Eager to leave home, she moved out at eighteen and married quickly. Her husband drank constantly, had affairs, and got into trouble with the law. At twenty-two, Joyce gave birth to a son and left her marriage, praying that God would give her someone who truly loved her and would bring her to church.

Not long after that, Joyce met Dave Meyer, who had been praying for a wife, and in particular, a woman who needed help. They were married January 7, 1967. Inspired by Dave's peace, joy, and stability, Joyce began walking with the Lord through the process of emotional healing. In 1976, she was filled with the Holy Spirit and began to study the Word of God more diligently. While making her bed one day, the Lord spoke to her heart, "You're going to go all over the place and teach My Word, and you're going to have a large teaching tape ministry." Joyce didn't know what a teaching tape ministry was, but her faith was greatly strengthened, and she committed herself to what God had called her to do.

**PERSONAL TOUCH**

*Each year, Joyce Meyer ministers to more than 200,000 people at her U.S. conferences alone. Joyce gives the people what they have grown accustomed to receiving through her worldwide television program—a poignant and practical message from God to help them enjoy their everyday life.*

## STEPPING OUT

For several years, Joyce taught a weekly Bible study in her home. In 1980, she became an associate pastor at Life Christian Center church in St. Louis. There she established a weekly meeting for women, and the meeting flourished.

In 1985 God called her to step out on her own, and she began holding conferences locally and eventually nationwide, bringing a message of restoration and hope. Her fifteen-minute local radio broadcast expanded to hundreds of stations. She aired her first television broadcast on September 19, 1993, and thousands were introduced to her straight talk and personal candor as she taught God's principles. Today, Meyer's *Enjoying Everyday Life* broadcast airs on hundreds of television and radio stations worldwide in more than twenty languages. In 2003, it began airing throughout the Middle East on the Life Channel, where it is dubbed into Arabic and reaches a potential audience of three hundred million. The program can be seen at www.joycemeyer.org.

Each year, two hundred thousand people experience Joyce Meyer in person at one of her many U.S. conferences. Dave and Joyce

**MINISTERING TO THE MASSES**

(above) Nearly one million people attended Joyce's open-air crusade in Hyderabad, India. Dave and Joyce have held conferences in several nations, including South Africa, the United Kingdom, and the former Soviet Union.

also travel internationally, holding large conferences in South Africa, the United Kingdom, and the former Soviet Union. Nearly a million people attended Joyce's four-day open-air crusade in Hyderabad, India.

Joyce has released more than 250 audio teaching series on a wide range of subjects, including emotional healing, freedom from fear, the battlefield of the mind, and more. Each year, Joyce Meyer Ministries (JMM) distributes 4.5

wells in third world countries, improving life for hundreds of thousands of people and introducing them to the gospel.

Meyer has foreign offices in Australia, India, Brazil, the United Kingdom, Canada, South Africa, the Middle East, and the former Soviet Union, and she has teamed with Children's Cup International and other mission groups to provide 3.5 million meals each year to the poor and hungry in places like Nepal,

**WATER OF LIFE**

(middle left) The Meyers dedicate a new church and well. To date, JMM has constructed and installed 175 churches and freshwater wells in third world countries.

**PROVIDING HOPE FOR CHILDREN**

(middle right) Dave and Joyce visit with orphans at one of their ministry-supported homes in Chennai, India. JMM fully funds and operates forty-one orphanages throughout Asia.

million teachings worldwide. Meyer has authored more than 70 books, most of them best sellers. Working with pastors and missionaries in various countries, JMM has distributed 7 million free copies of Joyce's titles in 63 foreign languages.

## A WORLDWIDE TOUCH

Meyer offers the love of Christ to millions each year through groundbreaking mission outreaches. JMM has constructed and installed 175 churches and freshwater

Thailand, Myanmar, Cambodia, and Swaziland. JMM fully funds forty-one orphanages. After the 2004 tsunami in Southeast Asia, JMM dispatched thousands of volunteers and distributed one hundred tons of food along with cooking utensils, fresh water, blankets, clothing, medicine, hygiene items, eyeglasses, and other necessities. The ministry rebuilt three villages in India and Sri Lanka, including three hundred new homes complete with electricity and running water. JMM also gave away hundreds of fishing

boats, bicycles, sewing machines, and motorized rickshaws to help people rebuild their businesses.

In 2000, JMM founded the St. Louis Dream Center, an inner-city church and outreach facility reaching thousands of helpless and hurting people in St. Louis. JMM has also gained unprecedented access to prisons to hand-deliver gift bags to inmates containing a letter from Dave and Joyce, a Joyce Meyer book, and soap and shampoo. The ministry has distributed a million hygiene bags to inmates in the United States and abroad.

In 2005, Joyce was named by *Time* magazine as one of the top twenty-five evangelical leaders in America. Today, Joyce's four children and their spouses hold significant leadership posts in JMM's operation.

Joyce Meyer is the first to say that only God could have brought her from where she was to where she is now. She remains committed to using her experiences and insights to help others find freedom by becoming established in God's Word.

**PROCLAIMING FREEDOM TO THE CAPTIVES**
*(above left) Dave and Joyce visit prisoners in the Louisiana State Penitentiary.*

**ON THE AIR**
*(above right) Joyce records her telecast with special guests Joel and Victoria Osteen.*

"Dave and I want to reach the world with the good news of the gospel and help as many people as we can. We have such a passion to help others develop a relationship with Jesus Christ and experience wholeness in every area of their lives. We are consumed with the desire to help hurting people."

—*Joyce Meyer*

# WORKING FOR A WORLD HARVEST

## ROD PARSLEY, WORLD HARVEST CHURCH

**W**ORLD HARVEST CHURCH IN COLUMBUS, OHIO, WAS FOUNDED BY ROD PARSLEY AS A BACKYARD BIBLE STUDY IN 1977 AND IS NOW ONE OF THE HIGHEST-PROFILE CHRISTIAN MINISTRIES IN THE UNITED STATES.

Parsley began his ministry as a teenage student at Circleville (Ohio) Bible College. The first Bible study he led in his parents' backyard drew seventeen people. Within two years, the group had grown large enough to construct a building on ten acres near Pickerington, Ohio. The congregation was known as Sunrise Chapel, and later Word of Life Church.

During the church's early period of growth, Parsley met evangelist Lester Sumrall, who became his mentor and spiritual father. When Parsley's church

**BLESSED BEGINNINGS**

*(top to bottom) The forerunner of World Harvest Church, called Sunrise Chapel, was located on 10 acres near Columbus, Ohio. The building is now part of the campus of World Harvest Bible College. The Bible college, founded in 1990, has drawn students from all 50 states and more than 30 nations. (illustration at right) Lester Sumrall passed the sword of anointing to Rod and Joni Parsley in 1992. Sumrall had received the anointing from Smith Wigglesworth.*

dedicated its current facility in 1987, they renamed it World Harvest Church in honor of Sumrall's ministry. In 1992 Sumrall passed his "sword of anointing" to Rod and wife, Joni, conferring on Rod the spiritual mantle of his ministry.

Today World Harvest Church meets in a 5,200-seat tabernacle, and the 300,000-square-feet complex includes a full-service cafeteria, conference rooms for up to 3,000 people, a three-court gymnasium, and a handicapped-accessible playground.

## WIDENING SCOPE OF MINISTRY

Parsley's broadcast ministry began in 1983 when he contracted with a television studio to begin producing *Promise*. When the studio went out of business, Parsley bought their equipment and has produced his program in-house ever since. His Breakthrough Media Ministry has experienced phenomenal expansion. The daily and weekly television program *Breakthrough* is available to 97 percent of American homes, 78 percent of Canadian homes, and nearly every nation of the world. It is translated into Spanish in thirty nations.

World Harvest Church's most recent outreach, the Center for Moral Clarity (CMC), has given Parsley a national platform to speak to crucial moral issues. CMC advocates for biblical solutions to political and social problems. As Parsley wrote in his 2005 best seller *Silent No More*, "I intend to speak boldly to both sides of the political spectrum: to both the believing and the nonbelieving."

In 2004, CMC took on its first significant project, a national voter registration drive carried out through the one thousand churches of the World Harvest Church Ministerial Fellowship and many other congregations. Parsley was a leading figure in successfully pushing for a state constitutional amendment in Ohio that defined marriage as

**BREAKTHROUGH AND HARVEST**
*(top to bottom) Breakthrough's World Ministry Center is nestled among cornfields in Columbus, Ohio. It includes Harvest Preparatory School, which features one of just three handicapped-accessible playgrounds in the metropolitan area.*
*Through the Center for Moral Clarity, founded in 2004, Parsley has become one of Christianity's most prominent spokesmen for issues of righteousness and justice. He is pictured with his wife, Joni.*

His desire remains that God would "do things so incredibly large and powerful through this ministry that people would have to say, 'No person could have done this.'"

**FREEING CAPTIVES**
*Through Bridge of Hope, World Harvest Church's missions outreach, Parsley has worked since 1999 to free thousands of former slaves in the African nation of Sudan and provide them with life-sustaining food and supplies.*

the union of one man and one woman. Parsley was interviewed on Fox News Channel, ABC's *World News Tonight*, and CNN. He has also been quoted in the *New York Times, Dallas Morning News, Washington Post, Time* magazine, and *USA Today*, and was a guest on CNN's *Larry King Live*.

In October 2005, Parsley launched Reformation Ohio, an organization of churches and ministries committed to a reawakening of the state's churches and revival among its citizens. Reformation Ohio will be the model for similar reformation efforts across the nation. Parsley founded Reformation Ohio and sits on its board with ministers, civic leaders, and business people from a variety of faith backgrounds. The organization's goals include presenting the gospel to one million Ohioans so at least one hundred thousand accept Christ; registering new voters; and completing compassion projects to bless families throughout the state. Youth With A Mission's Impact World Tour is a partner in Reformation Ohio.

## BRIDGE OF HOPE

Through Bridge of Hope missions, Parsley has given millions of pounds of supplies to nations like Nicaragua and Kosovo, and to victims of disaster in Venezuela, Mozambique, India, and El Salvador. Parsley was particularly moved by the plight of persecuted Christians in Sudan, and Bridge of Hope has provided life-saving relief to the Sudanese since 1999. Due in part to Parsley's efforts, the U.S. government passed the Sudan Peace Act in 2002.

**COMPASSION**

*Parsley, left, directed that Bridge of Hope's largest domestic relief effort be directed to America's Gulf Coast in September 2005. Victims of Hurricane Katrina and Hurricane Rita received two million pounds of food, water, and other essential supplies.*

Bridge of Hope also became the catalyst in freeing more than 18,400 Sudanese Christian slaves.

Bridge of Hope has distributed a million pounds of food in cities across America, including the impoverished region of Appalachia.

## EQUIPPING THE NEXT GENERATION

Parsley founded Harvest Preparatory School, a K–12 school and preschool, in 1986. More than 80 percent of HPS graduates go on to colleges and universities. In fall 2005, Parsley launched Harvest Prep Virtual Academy, an online school serving parents nationwide who want to give their children a Christ-centered, home-based education.

World Harvest Bible College, founded in 1990, sits on the church's original site. Students from all fifty states and more than thirty nations have attended the college.

After Sumrall's death in 1996, Parsley felt called to mentor and lead other men and women of God, so he responded by founding the World Harvest Church Ministerial Fellowship. The fellowship now counts more than 2,150 members, including more than 1,090 senior pastors, from all 50 states and 55 nations. Its membership encompasses a wide range of denominations and cultures.

Today, twelve thousand people attend World Harvest Church each week, and the church continues to grow in size and diversity. Parsley speaks widely in crusades and conferences. His desire remains that God would "do things so incredibly large and powerful through this ministry that people would have to say, 'No person could have done this.'"

**MINISTRY**

*More than 12,000 members and regular attendees call World Harvest their church home. The church also hosts Dominion Camp Meeting, Raise the Standard Pastors' and Church Workers' Conference, and other events.*

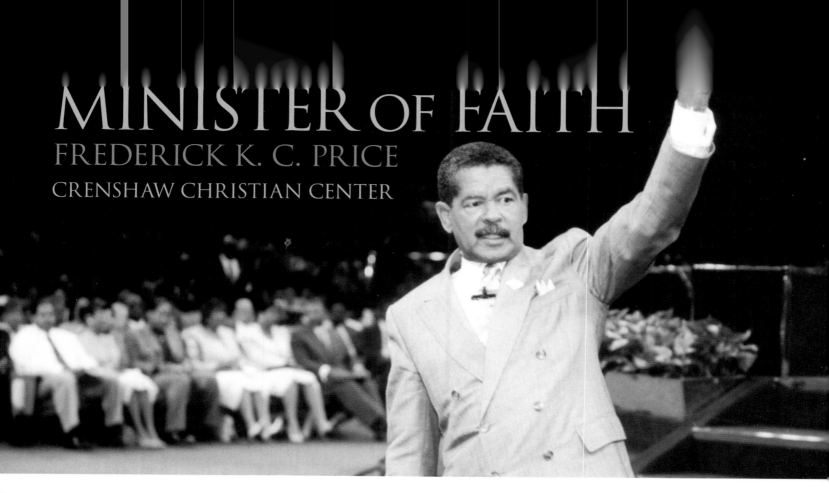

# MINISTER OF FAITH
## FREDERICK K. C. PRICE
### CRENSHAW CHRISTIAN CENTER

**T**HOUGH RAISED IN A NONRELIGIOUS HOUSEHOLD, FREDERICK K. C. PRICE WENT ON TO BUILD ONE OF THE GREAT CHURCHES AND MINISTRIES OF THE PAST HALF-CENTURY. HE PASTORS CRENSHAW CHRISTIAN CENTER, A MULTICULTURAL CONGREGATION THAT MEETS IN THE TEN-THOUSAND-SEAT FAITHDOME IN LOS ANGELES. PRICE'S EVER INCREASING FAITH MEDIA MINISTRY TOUCHES MILLIONS OF LIVES THROUGH RADIO, TELEVISION, AND BOOKS.

Price was born in 1932 in Santa Monica, California, and attended public schools and Los Angeles City College. His parents were Jehovah's Witness adherents who abandoned their faith when Price was very young. They did not join another church. Fred, an only child until his teenage years, essentially raised himself, even paying for his own cap and gown for his high school graduation.

**GROWING IN MINISTRY**
*(left) Interior and exterior views of the FaithDome.*
*(above, left to right) Fred and Betty Price at a Baptist church in 1954, and with their first two children when Fred was pastoring his first African Methodist Episcopal (AME) church in Val Verde, California.*

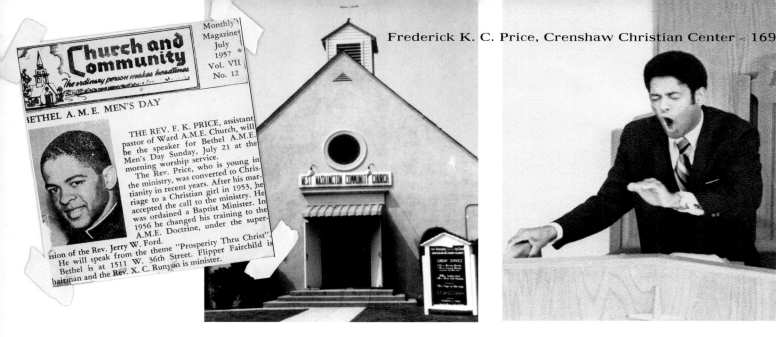

Church and Community
*The ordinary person makes headlines*

Monthly
Magazine
July
1957
Vol. VII
No. 12

BETHEL A. M. E. MEN'S DAY

THE REV. F. K. PRICE, assistant
pastor of Ward A.M.E. Church, will
be the speaker for Bethel A.M.E.
Men's Day Sunday, July 21 at the
morning worship service.
The Rev. Price, who is young in
the ministry, was converted to Christianity in recent years. After his marriage to a Christian girl in 1953, he
accepted the call to the ministry. He
was ordained a Baptist Minister. In
1956 he changed his training to the
A.M.E. Doctrine, under the super-
vision of the Rev. Jerry W. Ford.
He will speak from the theme "Prosperity Thru Christ"
Bethel is at 1511 W. 36th Street. Flipper Fairchild is
chairman and the Rev. X. C. Runyon is minister.

**BUILDING BY FAITH**
*(opposite page, top) Price
preaches in the FaithDome, a
10,000-seat sanctuary that is
home to the 22,000-member
Crenshaw Christian Center.
(above) An article ran in a
popular newspaper in 1957
when Fred spoke in an AME
church. (above, middle and
right) Later, Price pastored the
West Washington Community
Church, and is shown teaching
there in 1965.*

Price met Betty Ruth Scott, a devout
Baptist, while attending Dorsey High School
and feigned religious interest to woo her.
After they married in 1953, Fred refused
to go to church anymore. But one night
he followed Betty to a tent revival and was
saved. They joined a Baptist congregation.
There Price heard an audible voice saying,
"You are going to preach My gospel."

## TRANSFORMED BY THE SPIRIT

Over the next several years, Price struggled
to find satisfaction in his Christian walk. He
and Betty joined four different denominations
and pastored in three, but felt fulfilled in
none of them. In 1962 their eight-year-old
son, Frederick III, was struck and killed by
a car while coming home from school.

In June 1965, Fred became pastor of the
West Washington Community Church of the
Christian and Missionary Alliance, a church with
nine members. Because the pay was so low he
was forced to hold a full-time non-ministry job.

In four years West Washington's
congregation grew to nearly one hundred thirty
people, but Fred was not spiritually satisfied.
Inspired by the ministry of Kathryn Kuhlman,
he searched the Scriptures and concluded that
the Holy Spirit was the "missing ingredient"
in his life. He wept in the pulpit one Sunday

**EXPANSION**
*In the 1970s, Price taught in
Crenshaw Christian Center's
first church sanctuary in
Inglewood, California.*

> "When I first established the ministry that has come to be known as CCC, my sole purpose was to proclaim the good news of Jesus Christ and to teach the uncompromising Word of God according to the literal interpretation of the Bible. When I received the vision in my spirit of having a church of born-again, Spirit-filled believers governed solely by the principles recorded in God's Word, I determined that 'excellence of ministry,' worthy of the name of Christ, would be my primary aim."
>
> —Frederick K. C. Price

and vowed he would stop preaching if he didn't receive the Holy Spirit. Price did receive the gift of the Holy Spirit with the evidence of speaking with other tongues on February 28, 1970. As a result, nearly everyone in his congregation was baptized in the Holy Spirit as well, and the church was transformed.

The church was located on a dead-end street, set back from direct view, but attendance more than doubled. On Sunday mornings people formed a long line around the building to wait for the doors to open. Classrooms, the kitchen, bathrooms, even the platform itself were used to accommodate attendees, leaving Price a small area in which to teach.

At that same time Price discovered the teachings of Kenneth Hagin and the principles of faith, healing, and prayer. In 1973, Price and three hundred parishioners acted on faith and moved from West Washington to a fourteen-hundred-seat sanctuary in Inglewood. The facility was located at 9550 Crenshaw Boulevard, and they named the church Crenshaw Christian Center (CCC). News spread about the dynamic teachings of this young black minister, and the size of the congregation grew every week. Price made "excellence of ministry" his goal.

## MULTICULTURAL MEGACHURCH

CCC grew rapidly and bridged African American churches and the megachurch movement. By 1977 the congregation was four thousand members strong. In 1978 Price became the first black preacher to have an evangelical ministry broadcast on television. In 1982 he received an honorary doctorate of divinity degree from Oral Roberts University.

CCC purchased a thirty-two-acre former university campus in South Los Angeles in 1981 and constructed a sanctuary unprecedented in size and design. In September 1989 the ten-thousand-seat FaithDome was complete, one of the largest church sanctuaries in the United States. Today, CCC's membership totals twenty-two thousand people.

**LEAP OF FAITH**
(above) When the FaithDome was built in the early 1980s it was unprecedented in scope and design. Today it sits on thirty-two acres in South Los Angeles and hosts dozens of ministries, including an elementary school and Price's television ministry.

**HIP HOP OUTREACH**

*Fred and Betty Price's son, Frederick K. Price, founded a world-renowned Hip Hop Sunday ministry in August 2003. Services have drawn 7,000 people who attend church wearing hip hop gear and listen to gospel-inspired hip hop music. Hundreds have been led to Christ as a result of the special services.*

CCC now operates a preschool, K–12 school, and correspondence school. Price's *Ever Increasing Faith* television program reaches fifteen million households each week.

In 1990, Price founded the Fellowship of Inner-City Word of Faith Ministries (FICWFM), which provides fellowship, leadership, and guidance for inner-city ministries aiming for excellence. Membership now includes five hundred ministers worldwide representing thirty-eight states and seventeen foreign countries.

**FICWFM**
FELLOWSHIP OF
INNER-CITY
WORD OF FAITH
MINISTRIES

Price has authored fifty books on faith, healing, prosperity, and the Holy Spirit, including the classic *How Faith Works*. Price's books have sold 2.1 million copies. In 1997 Price gave a controversial teaching on "Race, Racism, and Religion" that aired on television for a year and produced a best-selling book and tape series. The controversial series shook the Christian community.

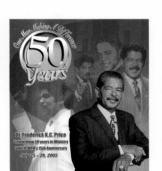

In 1998, Price received the Horatio Alger Award, which honors those who exemplify inspirational success. That year he also received the Kelly Miller Smith Interfaith Award, presented by the Southern Christian Leadership Conference. In 2001 he established Crenshaw Christian Center East in Manhattan, New York, with about one thousand members. All four of Price's children and sons-in-law work in his ministry.

With fifty years of ministry and integrity behind him, Price is more dedicated than ever to excellence in ministry and to training people in faith and in the power of God.

**A FAMILY OF MINISTERS**
*(left) The logo of the Fellowship of Inner City Word of Faith Ministries, which Price founded in 1990, and the cover of the 50th ministry year commemorative book given out at the FICWFM convention. (below) The Price family in 2002. All four of Fred and Betty Price's children and sons-in-law work alongside them in ministry. "This ministry will continue training people to go to the nations equipped with the power of God to make a difference," Price says.*

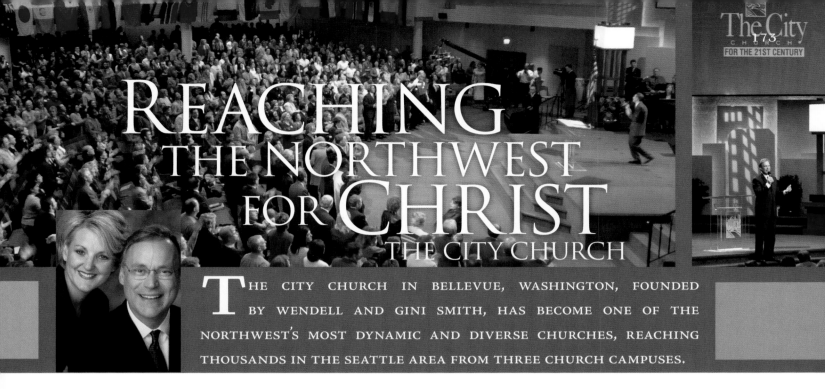

# REACHING THE NORTHWEST FOR CHRIST

## THE CITY CHURCH

**T**HE CITY CHURCH IN BELLEVUE, WASHINGTON, FOUNDED BY WENDELL AND GINI SMITH, HAS BECOME ONE OF THE NORTHWEST'S MOST DYNAMIC AND DIVERSE CHURCHES, REACHING THOUSANDS IN THE SEATTLE AREA FROM THREE CHURCH CAMPUSES.

The Smiths met at Northwest Nazarene University in Nampa, Idaho, married in 1972, and served for twenty years at City Bible Church (formerly Bible Temple) in Portland, Oregon. In the mid-1980s, the Smiths took their Dragonslayer Seminar to 100,000 young people across the nation.

Then Bible Temple sent the Smiths to launch The City Church in the Seattle area in 1992. The church started with forty people in a hotel conference room, then moved into a retail mall in Bellevue. By 1996, a thousand people attended every weekend.

In 1997, the church purchased a thirteen-acre complex with 111,000 square feet of building space. Services at the new location drew more than three thousand people.

Today The City Church has added two new campuses, one in downtown Seattle just blocks from the Space Needle, and the other on forty acres outside Seattle. Each campus participates in Sunday morning services live and by videoconference, creating one area-wide congregation.

The City Church places high priority on serving people of diverse ethnicities, ages, and denominational backgrounds. Through their City Ministries they help to feed more than twenty thousand people a week and supply one hundred fifty different churches with food for their communities.

Each week, fifteen hundred young people gather for dynamic Generation Church services. These are held at many locations, including the University of Washington campus. Generation Church produces its own weekly half-hour TV program.

The portion of Psalm 126 posted above the entry to the Kirkland campus sanctuary tells the on-going City Church story: "We laughed, we sang, we couldn't believe our good fortune. God was wonderful to us; we are one happy people."

**EARLY DEVELOPMENT**
*(top to bottom) One of the first official City Church Sunday services in 1992. The City Church's first true home at Kelsey Creek Center. The church later moved to Kirkland and an 111,000-square-feet building on 13 acres.*

**ONE CHURCH, THREE CAMPUSES**
*(below left) The City Church's home base is now called the Kirkland Campus.
(below middle) The Plateau campus is located on 40 acres, with a chapel, dormitories, and classrooms.*

**DIVERSITY**
*(top to bottom) The City Church's emphasis on vibrant, diverse ministry to children and young people is reflected in its City Kids ministry.
More than 1,500 young people gather every week for dynamic Generation Church services.*

**BRANCHING OUT**
*(below) The Belltown Campus, located in downtown Seattle, was The City Church's first satellite campus.*

The City Church

# PROCLAMING JESUS TO THE WORLD

## STRANG COMMUNICATIONS COMPANY

*Stephen Strang (c-1975) births the vision for* Charisma *magazine. The first issue, shown above, debuted in August 1975.*

**E**VERY MOVEMENT NEEDS A VOICE, AND SINCE 1975 *CHARISMA* MAGAZINE HAS CHRONICLED CHARISMATIC CHRISTIANITY, COVERING THE HIGHS AND LOWS OF THE WORLD'S LARGEST WAVE OF RENEWAL SINCE THE AZUSA STREET REVIVAL.

Stephen Strang, a fourth-generation Pentecostal whose grandmother was ordained in the Assemblies of God in 1914, was a reporter for the Orlando, Florida, newspaper when he first got the idea to launch a magazine that would track the work of the Holy Spirit around the world. The vision took form in 1975 when Strang convinced the leaders of his church, Calvary Assembly of God, in the Orlando area, to underwrite a "magazine about Spirit-led living," which he named *Charisma*. The first issue debuted in August of that year.

Though it was at first merely "a church magazine," it reported on national trends and issues. By the early 1980s, *Charisma* had become the primary source for what was happening in the Pentecostal-Charismatic community, replacing several earlier magazines that ceased publication.

Through the years *Charisma* has introduced many newcomers to a wider audience just as their ministries were beginning to become known. In 1979, the magazine profiled a popular radio Bible teacher named Marilyn Hickey and a relatively unknown Canadian evangelist named Benny Hinn. In more recent years, it introduced the ministries of leaders such as healing evangelists Charles and Frances Hunter, T. D. Jakes, and Randy and

Paula White. Through the years, *Charisma* has published cover stories or articles on every segment of the movement and every major leader.

In 1981 Strang set out on his own. Inspired by counsel from his friend and mentor Jamie Buckingham, who wrote *Charisma's* Last Word column from 1979 to 1993, Strang formed what is now called Strang Communications Company.

A pivotal point in the growth of the burgeoning publishing ministry was its "merger" in 1986 with *Christian Life* magazine founded by Robert Walker. In 1954, Walker, a leading evangelical, received the baptism in the Holy Spirit and gradually began covering events in *Christian Life*, such as when Pat Robertson, newly out of seminary, founded a tiny ministry called the Christian Broadcasting Network in 1960 or when singer Pat Boone was baptized in the Holy Spirit in 1969.

*An award-winning magazine and newspaper columnist, Jamie Buckingham was one of the most widely read Christian writers of his day. He founded and pastored the then 3,000-member Tabernacle Church of Melbourne, Florida. He was editor-in-chief of* Ministries Today *magazine and editor-at-large for* Charisma *magazine—and personal friend and mentor to Stephen Strang until his death in 1992.*

Strang has sought to continue Walker's legacy, and though he is well into his nineties, Walker still serves as editor emeritus for *Charisma and Christian Life.*

Today Strang Communications, based in Lake Mary, Florida, publishes eight magazines and has become a major publisher of both English and Spanish Christian books under various imprint brands focused on health, politics, fiction, children, and spiritual topics.

Recently the company has had a string of best sellers, including several on the *New York Times* best-sellers list.

At Strang Communications, publishing is a family affair. Strang's wife, Joy, not only serves as co-owner and CFO, but she also founded *SpiritLed Woman* magazine. The couple's oldest son, Cameron, along with his wife, Maya, own Relevant Media Group, which serves the twenty-somethings' generation by publishing *Relevant* magazine and cutting-edge books that reflect its motto "God. Life. Progressive Culture."

Through the years, *Charisma* has tackled a wide range of issues—addressing the problems of spiritual abuse during the discipleship movement of the 1970s, speaking out about integrity during the televangelism crisis of the late 1980s, challenging abortion during the Reagan and Clinton eras, and championing racial reconciliation in the 1990s. Along the way it also has encouraged denominational unity, expressed support for Israel, and championed the persecuted church.

In 2005, *Time* magazine recognized Stephen Strang as one of the nation's twenty-five most influential evangelicals, noting that he "combines a sense of mission with sharp business acumen." *Charisma* has even become prominent enough to wrangle an interview with President George W. Bush in 2004.

Strang's vision to "proclaim Jesus worldwide" not only includes an international distribution program, but it has also caused the company to launch initiatives into the secular arena, such as publishing the best seller *The Faith of George W. Bush* and distributing its magazines on secular newsstands.

Through its books, conferences, periodicals, and special events, Strang Communications has helped inform and unify Charismatic Christians around the globe. Some people think the company experienced overnight success, but Strang says the growth is the result of patience, tenacity, and faith. "It's not what I've done," Strang wrote in 2000 when *Charisma* celebrated its twenty-fifth anniversary. "It's, 'Look what the Lord has done.'"

*Left: Robert Walker, founder of Christian Life magazine, which merged with* Charisma *in 1986. Right: Strang Communications staff, taken in 2003.*

*Samples of current books and magazines published by Strang Communications.*

*Stephen Strang with his son Cameron Strang, president and CEO of Relevant Media Group, publishers of* Relevant *magazine and books for college students and twentysomethings.*

# BROADCASTING THE GOOD NEWS

## TRINITY BROADCASTING NETWORK

F ROM SMALL BEGINNINGS IN A RENTED STUDIO IN 1973, THE TRINITY BROADCASTING NETWORK (TBN), UNDER THE LEADERSHIP OF PAUL AND JAN CROUCH, HAS BECOME THE WORLD'S LARGEST RELIGIOUS NETWORK AND AMERICA'S MOST-WATCHED FAITH CHANNEL. BY SOME ESTIMATES IT IS THE SEVENTH LARGEST TELEVISION NETWORK OF ANY KIND IN THE WORLD. BILLIONS HAVE TUNED IN TO TBN, AND AT LEAST 25 MILLION PEOPLE HAVE COME TO FAITH IN JESUS THROUGH TBN'S MINISTRY.

## WHEN THEY BEGAN

TBN founder Paul Crouch was born in 1934 and raised in the home of missionary and pastor Andrew Crouch, one of the founders of the Assemblies of God fellowship. At age twelve, Paul began tinkering with a mass of radio wires and equipment in a friend's basement. At age fifteen, Crouch passed the Federal Communications Commission (FCC) test and became a licensed ham radio operator.

In 1952, Crouch attended Central Bible Institute in Springfield, Missouri, and formed an amateur radio club. After scrounging up tubes, condensers, resistors, and 50 watts of power, he founded KCBI, signing on with what would become his signature sign-on: "Hello, world!"

Crouch met Jan Bethany of Georgia in 1956 at a church in Rapid City, South Dakota. They married and became assistant pastors at First Assembly of God in Rapid City. The church could not fully support them financially, so Paul worked as a radio announcer at KRSD AM 1340, which eventually became

**EARLY BROADCASTS**
*(left) Paul Crouch at KCBI, the on-campus radio station he helped build at Central Bible College in Springfield, Missouri. (above) Paul on the set of the Assemblies of God TV and Film Production studio in Burbank.*

**READY TO LAUNCH**
*(right) Paul and Jan help ready the rented TBN studio for its first broadcast of the Praise the Lord program on May 28, 1973.*

KRSD-TV Channel 7. There Paul learned the basics of television broadcasting in what he described later as his boot-camp experience.

While serving as assistant pastors in Muskegon, Michigan, the Crouches received a call that would change their lives. Paul was told about a new TV and film production center being built in Burbank, California, by the Assemblies of God. He was offered the position of manager, which he accepted, and on Thanksgiving Day 1961, he, Jan, and their young two sons, Paul Jr. and Matthew, moved to California.

Crouch gained further experience managing radio and television stations for Ray Schoch, pastor of Faith Center Church in Glendale. Schoch's KHOF-TV Channel 30 was the first television station to devote its programming entirely to Christian television. Then, while driving out of the parking lot of Hollywood High School one night, Crouch heard the voice of God say, "I release you from your ministry at KHOF-TV." Crouch resigned and contacted the owner of KBSA-TV about the status of UHF station Channel 46. To Paul's surprise, Channel 46 had been off the air. Paul signed contracts, and three months later, on May 28, the TBN era was born.

*A photo from TBN's first Family Christmas TV special in 1973. Paul and Jan are pictured with sons Matt (left) and Paul Jr. The set was decorated with Christmas cards sent by TBN's early partners.*

## SUCCESS AND TRIALS

TBN first aired from Santa Ana, California, with one borrowed camera, two folding chairs, and a Sears shower curtain for a backdrop. Paul, Jan, and a dedicated group of volunteers scrambled to overcome financial and technical obstacles to get on the air. It was the initial fulfillment of a calling the Crouches had received just three months earlier—a vision to build a Christian television network that would some day take the gospel to the world.

By November 1973, more than three thousand people claimed salvation through TBN's ministry. Then, in late 1973, a pastor bought KBSA out from under Crouch. The fledging Trinity Broadcasting Network was about to come to an end, but after a time of agonizing prayer, Paul called a Southern California broadcaster who owned the license for Channel 40. The owner had decided to sell the license for Channel 40 that very day. Crouch purchased the station, and TBN was back on the air with four times the power and double the population coverage as before.

In August 1974 the Federal Communications Commission approved TBN's license, and in 1978 the FCC granted a permit that allowed TBN to broadcast its signal by satellite. Licensing, though, would be a continual struggle for TBN. In the 1980s the network was plagued by competing applications for its licenses and a license challenge from the FCC. Several times the future of the network hung in the balance, but in each case TBN prevailed.

**FIRST HOME**
*(above) TBN's first studio was located in a former computer office building in Santa Ana, California.*
*(below) On August 2, 1974, Paul picked up the Western Union telegram from the FCC granting TBN's first television license for Channel 40 in Southern California.*

**HOST AND PIONEER**
*(above) An early photo of Paul hosting the Behind the Scenes program. The table on the right was part of Paul and Jan's home bedroom set.*
*(left) In 1978, Paul, Jan, and hundreds of TBN partners prayed over and dedicated the new satellite station. TBN now reaches the world through its network of fifty-three international satellites.*

TBN grew during the 1980s and by 1994 had 450 stations and affiliates. The 1992 Cable Television Consumer Protection and Competition Act gave it the right to be carried on local cable systems, which meant access to millions more homes.

TBN was also quick to utilize new technologies. In 1995, TBN launched TBN.org, offering a constant presence on the World Wide Web. In 1996 the network began broadcasting on the Dish Network. The next year, DIRECTV added TBN to its service. In late 2004, TBN announced its shift from analog to digital television, a transition overseen by Paul Crouch Jr.

## TBN'S ORGANIZATION AND MISSION

TBN remains viewer supported, commercial free, and debt free. It operates a worldwide television network for a fraction of the cost of other U.S.-based networks, and with less staff. It provides programming for the entire family, based in values of faith in God, love of family, and patriotic pride. TBN programs appeal to a wide variety of viewers with gospel music concerts, talk shows, music videos, children's programs, health and fitness shows, and news and information programs.

After decades of building studios and transmission towers around the world, TBN is now upgrading its programming to include better movies, documentaries, music shows, concerts, Bible study programs, reality shows, and more. TBN founders Paul and Jan Crouch increasingly rely on their sons, Paul Jr. and Matt, to share the responsibilities of operating the network.

Matt Crouch produced *The Omega Code*, a top ten feature film on its opening weekend. TBN has since released other successful films like *Megiddo, The Revolutionary, The Emissary,* and *The Champion.*

**ACTION**

*In 1999, TBN's second full-length feature film,* The Omega Code, *was released. Paul is pictured with son, Matt, interviewing* Omega Code *star Michael York at the movie premiere in Hollywood.*

TBN recently launched four digital networks: JCTV, a youth network; The Church Channel, a multi-denominational religious network that features church service programs around the clock; TBN Enlace, a Spanish language network; and the Smile of a Child network, for children ages two to twelve.

TBN has also built several tourist attractions. Trinity Music City, USA in Nashville offers TBN-produced concerts, dramas, seminars, and special events. Virtual reality theaters at Trinity Music City, the

International Production Center in Dallas, TBN headquarters in Costa Mesa, and the newest virtual reality theater in Miami, all combine high-definition digital video technology with an exclusive forty-eight-channel digital audio system to showcase four original productions from TBN Films.

**SMILE OF A CHILD**

*Jan's ministry to children started in TBN's early days. Through her Smile of a Child outreach, she has distributed millions of toys to needy children worldwide, and is building hospitals in Haiti and Costa Rica.*

In the 1980s Jan Crouch visited Haiti and later founded Smile of a Child. What began as a humanitarian Christian feeding mission and toy drive has become a global outreach mission. Today, Smile of a Child touches the lives of tens of thousands of needy children throughout the world and is building hospitals in Haiti and Costa Rica.

TBN now reaches every major continent through fifty-three satellites and more than twelve thousand television stations and cable affiliates worldwide. The *Praise the Lord* program remains the heart and soul of the TBN program lineup, offering a steady variety of guests, including Christian pastors, political leaders, top athletes, war heroes, movie stars, and other entertainers. The vision born to Paul and Jan Crouch in a small studio in 1973 is still being fulfilled to the glory of God.

**HEADQUARTERS**

*(top to bottom) TBN's headquarters, Trinity Christian City International in Costa Mesa, California, is aglow with a million lights to celebrate the birth of Jesus—the Light of the world.*

*In 1997, Trinity Music City in Hendersonville, Tennessee, opened its doors. Formerly "Twitty City," home to country music star Conway Twitty, it is now a Christian tourist attraction featuring TBN-produced dramas, concerts, and special events, as well as the* Praise the Lord *program and virtual reality theater.*

**NEW TERRITORY**

*In 2001, Paul and Matt Crouch traveled to Baghdad, Iraq, to meet with pastors and Christian leaders. They are pictured on the parade grounds in front of Saddam Hussein's former Arch of Triumph.*

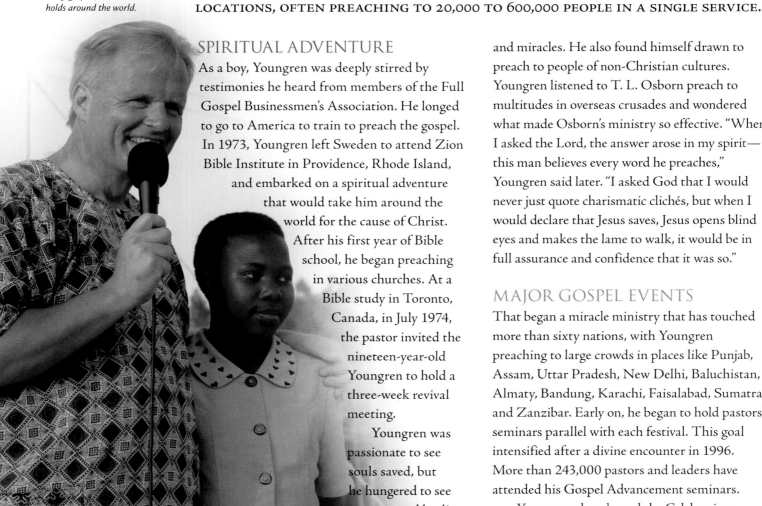

# GOING AFTER

## WIM PETER YOUNGREN
WORLD IMPACT MINISTRIES
One Savior for All People

**SAVED AND HEALED**
*Youngren with a girl who was healed at one of the many gospel festivals he holds around the world.*

PETER YOUNGREN, A NATIVE SWEDE, FOUNDED WORLD IMPACT MINISTRIES (WIM) IN 1976 TO BRING THE GOSPEL TO LARGE POPULATION CENTERS IN COUNTRIES AND CULTURES WHERE THE MESSAGE OF CHRIST IS NOT WELL KNOWN. HE HAS HELD MASSIVE GOSPEL FESTIVALS IN 150 LOCATIONS, OFTEN PREACHING TO 20,000 TO 600,000 PEOPLE IN A SINGLE SERVICE.

## SPIRITUAL ADVENTURE

As a boy, Youngren was deeply stirred by testimonies he heard from members of the Full Gospel Businessmen's Association. He longed to go to America to train to preach the gospel. In 1973, Youngren left Sweden to attend Zion Bible Institute in Providence, Rhode Island, and embarked on a spiritual adventure that would take him around the world for the cause of Christ. After his first year of Bible school, he began preaching in various churches. At a Bible study in Toronto, Canada, in July 1974, the pastor invited the nineteen-year-old Youngren to hold a three-week revival meeting.

Youngren was passionate to see souls saved, but he hungered to see supernatural healings and miracles. He also found himself drawn to preach to people of non-Christian cultures. Youngren listened to T. L. Osborn preach to multitudes in overseas crusades and wondered what made Osborn's ministry so effective. "When I asked the Lord, the answer arose in my spirit—this man believes every word he preaches," Youngren said later. "I asked God that I would never just quote charismatic clichés, but when I would declare that Jesus saves, Jesus opens blind eyes and makes the lame to walk, it would be in full assurance and confidence that it was so."

## MAJOR GOSPEL EVENTS

That began a miracle ministry that has touched more than sixty nations, with Youngren preaching to large crowds in places like Punjab, Assam, Uttar Pradesh, New Delhi, Baluchistan, Almaty, Bandung, Karachi, Faisalabad, Sumatra, and Zanzibar. Early on, he began to hold pastors' seminars parallel with each festival. This goal intensified after a divine encounter in 1996. More than 243,000 pastors and leaders have attended his Gospel Advancement seminars.

Youngren also planted the Celebration

# THE LOST

**THE POWER OF FAITH**
*Youngren at a festival in Bandung, Indonesia, where many were healed. "I asked God that . . . when I would declare that Jesus saves, Jesus opens blind eyes and makes the lame to walk, it would be in full assurance and confidence that it was so," Youngren says of the foundation of his ministry.*

than 50,000 people, including many Taliban supporters, gathered nightly. Newspapers and government leaders threatened to arrest Youngren and his team, but after notable miracles government leaders began to support the outreach.

## CROSS-CULTURAL MESSAGE

Youngren believes in a "front-door approach" to bringing the message of Christ to the highest office in the land. This has put him in contact with presidents and prime ministers, starting when he shared the gospel with the late Prime Minister Indira Gandhi in New Delhi, India, in 1982. WIM frequently holds friendship dinners with leaders of non-Christian religions to share the gospel.

Youngren and World Impact Ministries are advancing in key areas. Gospel festivals continue. More than 2,300 students have been trained at World Impact Bible Institute. Many graduates now run their own festivals, Bible schools, and church plants in places like Ethiopia, Indonesia, Kenya, and Tanzania. The Celebration Church plans to add several more preaching locations to expand its outreach.

Church in Ontario, Canada, which meets in two buildings, one in Niagara and one in Toronto, each seating between 1,500 and 2,000 people. The Niagara church is also home to World Impact Bible Institute, which draws students from many countries.

Christ's love has propelled WIM to the front lines of evangelism. While Mikhail Gorbachev was still president of the Soviet Union, Youngren held an open-air stadium crusade there. In 1991, around 200,000 people attended Youngren's meeting in the Central Square in Sofia, Bulgaria. In Quetta, near Afghanistan's border, more

Youngren is joined in his ministry by wife, RoxAnne, and their children. He believes America and the world are ready for a gospel revolution. Through expansion in the local church, gospel festivals, and television, Youngren's goal is to make the gospel known to all people in the power of the Holy Spirit.

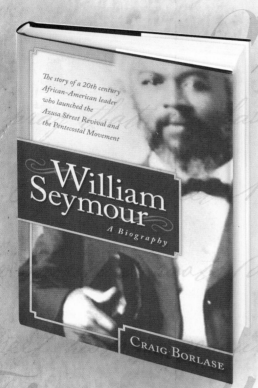
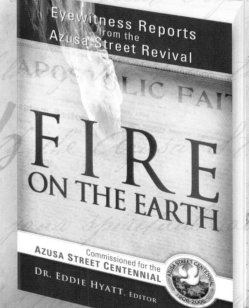

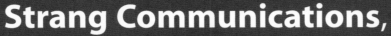